THE POCKET
ENCYCLOPEDIA
OF
GARDENING

THE POCKET
ENCYCLOPEDIA
OF
GARDENING

Abbeydale Press

This edition published in 2000 by
Abbeydale Press
An imprint of Bookmart Limited
Desford Road, Enderby
Leicester LE9 5AD
England

Originally published in 1993 by Bookmart Limited
as *The Practical Gardening Encyclopedia* and subsequently
in 1998 as *The Gardening Handbook*

Reprinted 2000

ISBN 1–86147–063–0

Printed and bound in Singapore

CONTENTS

FLOWERS & FOLIAGE 93

FRUIT & VEGETABLES 171

Gardening Basics

A garden does not look after itself, and if you want to get the best from your plants you have to think about the basics like watering, feeding, weeding, and pest and disease control. Fortunately, as the following pages show, these need not become onerous chores...and they are well offset by the delights to be discovered in the more 'creative' aspects of gardening such as propagation. Even pruning can be creative, as you learn to shape the shrubs as well as improve their flowering.

Opposite
Propagation is one of the most satisfying aspects of gardening, and if you have a greenhouse the scope is widened enormously.

INTRODUCTION

Gardening is a practical hobby that combines the art of design and the creative use of plants with the science of horticulture and the mechanics of garden construction.

Using the right tools always makes gardening easier, and whether beginner or not, the advice on choosing tools will get you off to a good start.

Adequate ground preparation is something that beginners in particular overlook, yet it can make the difference between success and failure. In the following pages you will find hints on testing and improving your

Above A weed-free lawn is as easy as watering, if you use one of the modern selective hormone weedkillers.

soil and advice on how to make good garden compost...something even experienced gardeners find difficult to achieve.

Few plants will thrive without feeding and watering, and there are practical tips on how to take the hard work out of both chores.

Pests are part of gardening and even expert gardeners get them. You will find advice on how to deal with some of the most common problems, with an organic solution as well as chemical.

You will find all the major propagation techniques described in easy-to-follow steps.

Above Paving stone paths can be interesting if you use your imagination and mix materials. Beach pebbles are used here to vary the texture.

Left Hand weeding is still needed, close to other plants.

Below Lawns benefit from a neat edge, and lawn edging.

Pruning is the one task that newcomers tackle with the most trepidation. The section on pruning removes the mystique, reducing the problem to a few common-sense steps that cover the majority of shrubs.

Some construction work is inevitable. Even if you are a newcomer to gardening, you will find here all the information you need for basic garden construction jobs.

Above centre Keep on top of pests and diseases.

Above Propagation can be as simple as pegging down shoots.

Left Pruning will keep roses in shape and flowering well.

CHOOSING TOOLS 1: DIGGING AND CULTIVATING TOOLS

Good quality, well-designed tools will often make a job much easier and remove some of the hard work.

Spade

Fork

SPADES

Choose a spade with a long handle if you are tall, and stainless steel blade if you can afford it.

• A D-shaped hilt provides good grip, but make sure your hand fits with a gardening glove on.

• Choose a full-sized blade if there's a lot of digging to do, or a border spade if planting trees and shrubs.

• A tread on top of the blade makes feet less tired, but the spade heavier.

• Wooden shafts are strong and comfortable, metal shafts should be plastic coated.

FORKS

A garden fork is invaluable for digging and lifting manure and compost.

• A D-shaped hilt is stronger than a Y-shaped one and more widely available than T-shaped hilts.

• Choose a full-sized head with square prongs, for general cultivation.

HOES AND RAKES

A hoe is one of the basic gardening tools ideal for keeping down weeds.

• The Dutch hoe is excellent for weeding between rows and around plants. Its angled head is designed to slice

Left: special trowel designed to fit into separate handle. Centre: traditional hand trowel and fork. Right: narrow trowel, used for rock gardens

Left: weeding trowel. Centre: patio/paving weeder. Right: daisy grubber

Left: draw hoe. Centre: proprietary three-bladed hoe. Right: Dutch hoe

through the weeds with minimum damage to plant roots.
• Choose a long handle so that you have less bending to do.
• An angled hoe has an angled head for taking out flat-bottomed drills for seeds and for drawing up earth around crops such as potatoes.
• Patent hoe designs sometimes have a smaller blade that cuts on more than one side for working close among plants.

A rake is useful in a kitchen garden and for making a new garden.

• Choose a long handle so that you have less bending to do.
• Buy a head that is made in one piece. Riveted heads are not so strong.

HAND CULTIVATORS AND WEEDERS

Hand cultivators are useful for breaking up the ground after digging, and for weeding between rows of seedlings or small plants.
• A cultivator that has removable prongs is more versatile than a fixed-prong type.
• Choosing one with a long handle that can be used with other heads and accessories can be useful.

Special tools are available for grubbing out daisies and other lawn weeds. These are useful, but worth buying only if you have regular use for them.

HAND FORKS AND TROWELS

Trowels are inexpensive and indispensable—you will need them for planting, but they are good for weeding and filling pots and containers.
   You can manage without a hand fork, but it is useful for weeding and loosening soil.
• A wide-bladed trowel is best for planting and general use around the garden.
• A narrow blade is good for confined areas, such as rock gardens.
• When buying a hand fork, make sure that the prongs are strong and the head is firmly fixed to the handle part.

Left: conventional rake. Above: a proprietary rake design

Hand weeder, also called a hand grubber

13

CHOOSING TOOLS 2: MOWERS

Almost every gardener owns a mower, but it is important to choose the most appropriate type for your garden.

Hover rotary mower

WHICH MOWER?

Manual mowers are worth considering for a very small garden.

Side-wheel mowers with no roller attachment are the lightest and easiest to use.

Rear-roller mowers are the best choice for a small lawn and a striped finish.

Wheeled rotary electric mowers are the choice for a medium sized lawn if you do not need a striped finish. For a large lawn, where a trailing cable could be a hazard, a petrol cylinder mower is a better choice.

Hover rotary mowers are useful for cutting awkward places, beneath branches and shallow slopes. They are lightweight and easy to manoeuvre.

Although not all rotary mowers have rear rollers or grass boxes, some have both these features. Shop around to see what is available.

Manual mower

Wheeled rotary electric mower

Rear-roller mower

SHARPENING

You can sharpen mower blades yourself, but it is best to have them done professionally. Rotary mower blades are not expensive to replace. Some can be fitted with plastic safety blades, and you might want to consider using these.

ELECTRICAL SAFETY

Check cables and plugs on electric mowers for damage or loose connections. Do this at the beginning of each season. If you do not have an earth leakage circuit in your house wiring, buy a special power point which has one fitted.

GETTING THE BEST FROM YOUR MOWER

Clean the blades after mowing. Remove any grass on other parts of the mower. Always disconnect the power supply to an electric mower before cleaning.

Adjust the cutting height throughout the year. Cut high in spring, then reduce the height gradually. The adjustments on your mower may vary from the

mower illustrated—consult your manual. Rotary mowers can also be adjusted for height of cut. See the manual for the correct method.

Adjust the blades of a cylinder mower so that it cuts evenly. Use a sheet of paper to check it cuts cleanly along the length of the blade. Rotate the cylinder slowly as you move the paper.

Make any necessary adjustments to the blade setting. Your mower may differ, so consult the handbook for your particular machine.

At the start of the season, and every month or so, put a drop of oil on bearings and chains. This will make the mower much easier to push.

WINTER WORK

Drain the petrol and oil from a petrol mower before you put it away for the winter.

Clean and replace the spark plug. Check your handbook for the correct gap setting.

Before replacing the spark plug, pour a tablespoon of oil into the cylinder and turn the engine over about half a dozen times.

Wipe the mower with an oily rag, or spray with an anti-rust before storing.

Before storing a rotary petrol or electric mower, clean the metal blades with an emery cloth.

Wipe the blade over with an oily rag to prevent rust. If the blade is worn, replace it.

Choosing Tools 3:
Trimming and Pruning Tools

Hedge-trimming is one of the most labour-intensive jobs in the garden. Electric hedge-trimmers make light work of the task, but hand shears may be better for a short hedge or trimming shrubs.

HEDGE-TRIMMERS

The longer the cutting length, the quicker you will cut the hedge. The longest blades are found on heavy machines. A 40cm (16in) blade is suitable for a small or medium-sized garden, but if you have a lot of hedges in a large garden, a 60cm (24in) blade will save a lot of time.

• A double-sided cutting edge is useful to cut in both directions.

• If both blades move vibration is likely to be much less. This is called reciprocal action.

• The more teeth there are for a given blade, the finer the finish will be.

• Blade extensions or guards, reduce the risk of injury.

• A hand shield should be included with the hedge trimmer.

• A lock off switch makes accidental starting less likely.

HAND SHEARS

Hand shears must be kept sharp and the pivots or bearings oiled, to reduce the physical effort required.

• Make sure that the blades are easy to adjust.

• Most shears have straight blades.

• A thick-shoot notch in the blade is useful if you have to cut through a thick shoot.

Hedge-trimmer with double cutting edge and blade guards

Secateurs: the two on the left have a by-pass action, the one on the right an anvil action

Long-handled pruners, sometimes called loppers

Handles are less important than the blades. Their shape has little bearing on the ease with which the shears are used.

SECATEURS

• Anvil secateurs cut when a sharp blade is held against a flat anvil. The anvil may have a groove to allow sap to run away. They will tear or crush stems if not kept well sharpened.

• By-pass secateurs have a scissor-like action, and produce a sharp, clean cut.

• Brightly coloured handles make the tool easier to see.

• The safety catch should be easy to use.

• Make sure the spring does not hold the blades too wide apart.

LONG-HANDLED PRUNERS

These are sold under a variety of names, such as loppers and branch cutters, but all do the same job: cutting through shoots and branches too thick or high up, for ordinary secateurs.

• By-pass blades may be easier to use in small spaces.

• Long handles have more leverage, so less effort is needed for thick branches.

Tree pruner

CHOOSING TOOLS 4: OTHER USEFUL TOOLS

There are newer tools for specific jobs, such as shredding waste or raking moss from lawns. Some of the most useful are described here.

NYLON-LINE TRIMMERS

These are the equivalent of the scythe, but are more versatile. Use them to trim long grass around trees or up to the edges of fences or walls. Brushwood cutters are more powerful machines, suitable for tough undergrowth, having metal discs.

• Cutting guides keep the line off the ground and prevent ground scalping.

• Two handles control the trimmer better and an adjustable shaft handle makes manoeuvring easier.

• An automatic line feed is useful.

• A swivel head allows the trimmer to edge a lawn.

SHREDDERS

Shredders are useful if you like to recycle as much garden refuse as possible, but their cost is usually justified only if you have a lot of waste to shred.

Shredders chop or mash woody and soft material so that it rots down more easily on the compost heap.

• The outlet spout should be high enough off the ground to slide containers below it.

Lawn rake

Traditional spring-tined lawn rake

- The inlet funnel should be large to use easily— but you should not be able to touch any moving parts.
- Wheels are very useful as shredders are heavy, and electric models cannot be left outside unprotected.

LAWN RAKES

These are good for raking out moss and 'thatch' (dead grass and debris) from a lawn. They are also useful for scattering worm casts and raking up autumn leaves.

- There are many kinds of manual lawn rakes, but the traditional fan-shaped spring-tined rake is the most useful.
- Powered lawn rakes save a lot of time on a large lawn, collecting leaves and debris.
- The wider the machine, the more expensive it is likely to be, but on a large lawn this saving in time will make it worthwhile.

Half-moon edgers, sometimes called edging irons

EDGING TOOLS

If you have a large lawn with a lot of edges, a half-moon edger (also called an edging iron) could be useful. It is used against a straight-edged piece of wood to straighten an uneven edge.

Although useful, over-use will gradually make your lawn smaller and beds and borders bigger!

Use long-handled edging shears or a nylon-line trimmer with a swivel head to trim grass overhanging the edge. If the edge keeps breaking down, use metal or plastic edging strips to reduce the problem.

Flymo

Nylon line trimmer

PREPARING THE GROUND 1

Digging helps to aerate the soil and expose pests to predators, and gives you the chance to incorporate humus-forming manures or garden compost. For heavy clay soils it can also help to improve the structure. The autumn and early winter is the best time for digging, but you can finish it off in the spring.

SINGLE DIGGING

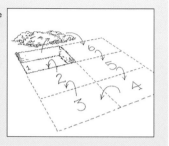

1 If you have a large area to dig such as a vegetable plot, or a new garden to cultivate, divide it into two equal areas. Then you can dig to one end and work back down the other side to finish where you began.

2 **Above** Remove a trench the width and depth of a spade.

3 **Above right** Push the spade into the soil at right angles, no more than a spade's width away from the previous bite of soil.

4 **Right** Push the spade in parallel to the trench, taking a bite about 15–20cm (6–8in) deep. Do not take larger bites as they will be too heavy to lift.

5 Pull back on the handle, using it as a lever to loosen the bite of soil, which will pull free on to the blade.

6 Lift the soil and flick the spade over to bury the weeds. At the end of a row, work back again in the opposite direction.

DIGGING A SMALL AREA

For a small area of ground in the garden, don't bother to divide the area. Just throw the soil forward as you work, then rake it level when preparing the ground for sowing or planting.

PERENNIAL WEEDS

If the soil is inverted properly, most annual weeds will be killed and will decompose to add humus to the soil. Remove the roots of troublesome perennial weeds by hand to prevent their spread.

7 When you reach the end of the plot, fill in the last trench with soil from the first row of the return half.

8 When you have dug the last row, fill in the trench left with the soil excavated from the first trench.

USING A GARDEN FORK

Use a spade for normal digging, but choose a fork to loosen ground that has already been dug recently. A fork is less likely to slice through the roots to leave pieces behind, and by shaking the prongs it is easier to remove difficult weeds.

Loosen the roots with a fork.

Pull up the roots by hand.

21

PREPARING THE GROUND 2

When planting or sowing seeds, you need to break down the soil to a fine tilth, after digging it and removing weeds. Fine, crumbly soil is essential if you are sowing seeds. For a lawn or an area where appearance is important, you may need to level the surface too.

PRODUCING A FINE TILTH (STRUCTURE)

1 Remove any large weeds that have been missed when digging. All the weed roots must be completely removed or they will regrow.

2 If the initial digging was done in the autumn, then go over the ground again, if planting in spring. A fork will open up the soil revealing any weeds.

LEVELLING WITH PEGS

1 Paint or mark 15cm (6in) long pegs 12–25mm (0.5–1in) from the top. Make sure that all the pegs are marked in exactly the same position.

2 Level the ground roughly. Insert a row of pegs about 1m (1yd) apart and check that the painted mark is at soil level.

3 Insert another row of pegs 1m (1yd) away from the first row. Use a spirit level in more than one direction to check all pegs are at the same height.

4 Repeat the process until the whole area has been pegged. Rake the soil, making sure that it is at the same level on each peg.

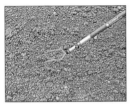

3 A hand cultivator is good for breaking down large clods of earth and doing some of the initial levelling.

4 Use an ordinary garden rake for the main levelling and smoothing, raking first in one direction and then another.

5 A combination of rake and hoe, produces a fine soil structure for a seed bed. A star-wheeled cultivator like this makes the job easier.

Seeds need a light, fine soil if they are to flourish.

TESTING YOUR SOIL

You can't determine how acid or alkaline your soil is, or how rich or deficient in nutrients, just by looking at it. Simple and inexpensive soil-testing kits will give you quick results, but they are not as accurate as a laboratory test.

TESTING FOR MAJOR NUTRIENTS

1 Gather your soil sample, using a trowel, from 5–8cm (2–3in) below the surface. Take samples from around the garden and test each one separately.

2 Mix 1 part soil to 5 parts water and shake in a clean jar, then allow to settle — this may take from half an hour to a day to become almost clear.

3 Slowly draw off some clear liquid from the top of the mixture for the test, using a pipette.

4 Using the pipette, transfer the solution to the test and reference chambers of the plastic container.

5 Add the powder from the capsule provided into the test chamber. Replace the cap and shake vigorously until the powder has dispersed.

6 Wait for the colour to develop, then compare the result against the chart which accompanies the kit. It will then tell you how to correct any problems.

APPLYING LIME

1 Try not to handle lime unnecessarily. Use gloves and goggles when applying it. Divide the area into 1m (1yd) squares and weigh out the correct amount. Apply with a spade, sprinkling evenly.

2 Use a rake to cover the lime and work it into the ground.

HOW MUCH LIME?

Use the following table as a guide to the amount of lime needed to raise the pH of your soil by 1pH. It is better to make several smaller applications over time than one big dose. Test the soil again after a month, and apply more lime if needed.

Do not apply lime at the same time as manure. There could be a reaction and nitrogen released can harm nearby plants.

TYPE OF SOIL	HYDRATED LIME	GROUND LIMESTONE
CLAY	640g/m² (18oz/yd²)	850g/m² (24oz/yd²)
AVERAGE LOAM	410g/m² (12oz/yd²)	550g/m² (16oz/yd²)
SAND	200g/m² (6oz/yd²)	275g/m² (8oz/yd²)

Chemicals which make the soil more acid do not produce a satisfactory result. It is better to grow plants suited to the soil you have. For the vegetable plot, adding garden compost or manure will raise the acidity by about 1pH.

A HANDY TEST

If you are unsure what type of soil you have try the following test:
- Pick up a handful of damp soil and rub it in your hand. If it feels gritty and is difficult to roll into a ball, it is sandy.
- If it is gritty but can be rolled into a ball, it is a sandy loam.
- If it is gritty or sticky and can be rolled into a cylinder, it is sandy clay loam or a clay loam.
- If you can bend the cylinder into a ring, it is clay.

PROBE METER

Meters are even quicker to use than indicator kits, but they need to be used carefully as instructed. Keep the probe clean, some recommend using fine emery paper to do this.

Push the probe into the soil and after a few moments read the pH on the dial. Repeat in different areas to get a consistent reading.

TESTING THE pH

The pH test is different as you don't have to wait for the soil/water mix to settle and only the test chamber is filled with this solution. Fill the reference chamber with clean tap water.

IMPROVING YOUR SOIL

Healthy vegetables are a good indicator of the condition of your soil.

All soils benefit from adding plenty of garden compost or well-rotted manure. Clay soils improve with drainage.

CREATING A SUMP

It is possible to drain the land into a natural drain or ditch, if allowed. If not make a sump in a low part of the garden and place drains so that water flows into it. The soakaway must be at least 60cm (2ft) deep and filled with rubble, topped with inverted turves and a layer of soil.

LAYING LAND DRAINS

1 Dig the trench at least 30cm (1ft) deep and at a slight fall. Put a layer of coarse grit or fine gravel along the bottom.

2 Both clay or plastic drains can be used satisfactorily. Lay the drains on the bed of gravel or grit.

SOIL CONDITIONERS

1 Dig in plenty of compost, manure or any organic matter that will quickly rot down in the soil. Peat and sharp sand will not rot down but improve the soil structure, aid drainage and moisture retention.

2 If the area has already been planted, use plenty of mulch material. This will eventually be worked into the soil.

3 Clay soil can be improved by applying lime and digging in coarse sand or grit. Concentrate on one area at a time. Also add plenty of compost or well-rotted manure.

3 Use a T shaped connector for side drains.

4 Pack coarse sand or fine gravel around the drains to improve drainage further and reduce the chance of the pipes becoming clogged.

MAKING GARDEN COMPOST

Garden compost is always valuable so make as much as you can. It is best to buy a bin or compost maker, or make one from scrap wood.

CONSTRUCTING A WOODEN BIN

1 The simplest way is to buy a kit. The wood is precut, ready to assemble by slotting the pieces together, or by nailing the slats to the corner pieces provided.

2 The kit above is quick and easy to make. The pieces are hammered into the slots forming a sturdy bin. Once full, simply lift the entire bin away and start a new compost heap.

READY-MADE COMPOST BINS

A proprietary compost bin with lid.

This bin is suitable for compost or leaves.

MAKING COMPOST

1 To improve airflow, place twiggy material at the bottom, then add kitchen and garden refuse.

2 Adding a layer of manure after every 15cm (6in) will speed up the rotting process.

3 A thin layer of soil can be substituted instead of manure which will add bacteria into the heap.

4 Compost activators will help speed up the rotting process by encouraging bacteria to grow. This will not be needed if manure has been added to the compost.

FERTILIZERS AND MANURES 1

Most gardeners use a combination of organic and inorganic fertilizers, some prefer the organic-only approach. Feeding does make a difference, especially to vegetables, seedlings and plants grown in containers. The benefits to trees and shrubs is less obvious, so feed only in response to a known deficiency.

1 Apply fertilizers evenly. Divide unplanted ground into strips 90cm (3ft) wide, work along these in 90cm (3ft) 'bites', scattering the fertilizer. A wheeled fertilizer spreader will do the job well.

2 Raking in the fertilizer, distributes it evenly as well as working it into the soil.

3 Scatter fertilizer either side of the vegetable rows, keeping it off the leaves. Hoe in later.

4 Scatter fertilizer in a circle around shrubs and large plants. This concentrates it where the active feeding roots are. Keep away from the stem, and do not apply beyond the spread of the plant.

5 Hoe in the fertilizer so that it penetrates more rapidly. Water in thoroughly, unless rain is forecast, so that the plants benefit more quickly.

INORGANIC FERTILIZERS

Ammonium Sulphate supplies nitrogen, but makes the soil more acid.

Nitro-chalk supplies nitrogen without making the soil more acid.

Potassium sulphate supplies potassium.

Superphosphate of lime supplies phosphorus. Triple superphosphate is similar but almost three times stronger. Make sure that you apply the correct lime at an appropriate rate.

Balanced fertilizers (such as Growmore in the UK— a formulation, not a trade name) contains all the main nutrients: nitrogen, phosphorus and potassium.

Compound fertilizers are usually the same as balanced fertilizers, but do not contain all three major nutrients.

Controlled- and slow-release fertilizers contain the major nutrients in a form that is released slowly over a period of months. Controlled-release fertilizers are regulated by the temperature of the soil.

Ammonium sulphate

Nitro-chalk

Potassium sulphate

Superphosphate of lime

Compound fertilizer

Slow-release fertilizer

Growmore

FERTILIZERS AND MANURES 2

GARDENING BASICS

Organic gardeners prefer to use fertilizers that occur as natural products.

ORGANIC FERTILIZERS

Blood, fish and bonemeal contains all the major nutrients. The nitrogen content is released quickly.

Bonemeal is a slow-acting fertilizer containing mainly phosphorus and nitrogen. Unsterilized bonemeal carries a very small risk of disease.

Dried animal manures contain a full range of trace elements but only a small amount of the major nutrients.

Dried blood is a fast-acting nitrogen fertilizer, when plants need a quick boost in summer.

Fish meal contains nitrogen and phosphorus.

Hoof and horn contains nitrogen in a form that is released slowly. It is a more suitable source of nitrogen than dried blood.

Liquid animal manures contain a small amount of all the major nutrients, plus a full range of trace elements.

Liquid seaweed contains a useful amount of nitrogen and potassium, but only a trace of phosphorus. Good for supplying trace elements and growth hormones.

Seaweed meal contains all the major nutrients, plus many minor ones and trace elements. It is a very good all-round fertilizer, but is best applied when the soil is warm so that the bacteria can break it down.

Wood ash the exact chemical analysis depends on the material burned, but there will be a useful amount of potassium and a small amount of phosphorus.

BULKY MANURES AND COMPOST

Garden compost, well rotted animal manures and bulky organic materials are invaluable. They improve the soil structure, its water holding capacity and the ability of the soil to retain nutrients from other sources.

Dried chicken manure

Blood, fish and bonemeal

Bonemeal

Dried blood

GREEN MANURING

1 Green manuring is a way of adding humus to the soil without making a compost heap. Fork over the cleared ground first of all.

2 Scatter mustard seed, covering the ground quite thickly.

3 Rake over to bury the mustard seed completely.

4 When the mustard is 30cm (12in) high, and before it flowers and sets seed, dig it into the ground. It will eventually rot, releasing humus and nutrients for a later crop.

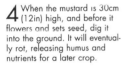

Liquid seaweed

Seaweed meal

Fish meal

Hoof and horn

WATERING

Watering by hand is hard work but an automatic watering system will eliminate that and be better for the plants.

DRIP FEEDS

1 A system like this will run both spray and drip nozzles off the same system. Connect the master unit to a hose from the mains. The master unit reduces water pressure and contains a cleanable filter.

2 Run the main supply tube so it is not too visible.

4 Use drip-feed heads to water containers and individual plants in borders. Pegs hold the tubes in position.

3 Connect the smaller-diameter branch tubes wherever you need to take water.

5 Use a spray head for more general watering in flower beds or vegetable plots. Various sizes of nozzles are available.

CHOOSING AN APPROPRIATE SPRINKLER

Oscillating sprinklers are useful for rectangular lawns and seed beds as they are adjustable.
Static sprinklers are intended mainly for lawns, generally watering in a circular pattern, so moving them around is necessary to achieve an even coverage.

Rotating sprinklers water in a circular pattern. The rotating arms throw out droplets by water pressure and cover a wider area than static sprinklers.

To water a flower bed or vegetable plot, you will need to buy a version with a head on a long spike.

Pulse-jet sprinklers have a single jet on a central pivot that rotates in a series of pulses, ejecting a spurt of water. They water in a circular pattern but can cover a very wide area. Lawn versions have a low base.

Oscillating sprinkler

Static sprinkler

Rotating sprinkler

Pulse-jet

TAPS AND TIMERS

An outdoor tap is essential if you have a drip-feed watering system. Kits are readily available with fitting instructions. In the UK a non-return valve must be fitted by law.

If you have installed an automatic watering system, consider installing a tap computer to turn the water supply on and off automatically.

SEEP HOSES

Seep hoses are designed for long-term watering. The tiny perforations deliver the water slowly so that it seeps down into the soil. Use in flower beds, borders or rows of fruit or vegetables.

SEEPAGE HOSE

Some seepage hoses are made of porous rubber and can be laid on top of the soil or buried in a shallow slit trench 10–15cm (4–6in) deep.

WEEDING BEDS AND BORDERS

Weeds look unsightly and can affect the growth of your plants by competing for water and nutrients. Once you have a plan of action, weeding should be no more than an occasional chore.

HAND-WEEDING

1 Some hand weeding is always necessary, but forking out deep-rooted perennials need only be done when you are clearing the ground. Use a fork to loosen the roots so that the whole root system is removed.

2 Hand forking will control perennial weeds while they are still young.

3 Hoeing, in dry weather, keeps most weeds under control. A Dutch hoe, like this, is good for slicing off the tops of weeds. Other designs are available.

4 A hand cultivator with removable prongs is good for loosening the soil and weeds in the vegetable plot. They are not good at slicing off the tops of weeds.

CHEMICAL WEEDING

1 The quickest way to clear the ground of weeds, is to use a chemical weedkiller. Choose the correct weedkiller for the job and area of the garden.

Spray on a calm day so no spray drifts onto plants or grass. Keep one watering can especially for weedkillers and label it clearly.

2 Most weedkillers act quickly within days. Some products are inactivated by contact with the soil, allowing planting as soon as dead growth is cleared. Translocated weedkiller acts to kill difficult perennial weeds, and once top growth is dead the weed can be removed.

3 Where spraying is impossible, paint a translocated weedkiller (such as a glyphosphate) on to individual weeds.

MULCH CONTROL

1 Black polythene sheets controls weeds effectively in areas of no importance. It can be secured with soil or pegs or weighed down with bricks.

2 In areas where appearance matters, cover any bare ground with a 5cm (2in) layer of chipped bark or other decorative mulch.

PREPARING THE GROUND 1

A weed-free lawn or path is no longer a dream with the selective weedkillers available today. They attack the weeds but not the grass so you can achieve a superb lawn and clear paths with just one or two applications.

LAWN WEEDKILLERS

1 Most selective lawn weedkillers are diluted and applied as a liquid. To ensure even coverage, use two lengths of string to mark out the width of the dribble bar used with your watering can.

2 At the end of a row, move one of the strings across for the next strip. Always carefully follow the instructions for the rate of coverage.

3 If the lawn also needs feeding, use a weed-and-feed for lawns. This combines fertilizer and weedkiller and can be applied with a fertilizer spreader to save time.

4 If there are isolated weeds in small patches, do not apply weedkiller to the whole lawn. Use instead a wipe-on stick containing a selective weedkiller, applied directly onto the weeds.

HAND-WEEDING A LAWN

DEALING WITH COARSE GRASS

Small clumps of coarse grass growing in your lawn can either be dug up and the area reseeded, or keep slashing through it with a knife. This will weaken it allowing fine grasses to grow over the area.

1 Weeding trowels are useful for prising up weeds such as dandelions and daisies.

2 Firm the soil afterwards to prevent seedlings germinating in the area. If a large bare area is exposed, it is worth sprinkling grass seeds over the patch.

PATH WEEDKILLERS

1 Path weedkillers kill all plants that they touch, remaining active in the soil for months. Great care should be taken to avoid spray blowing onto plants or grass.

2 Shield plants with a sheet of board, wood or plastic if applying weedkiller near a border.

PEST CONTROL 1:
APHIDS AND OTHER SAP-SUCKERS

Sap-sucking insects weaken the plants they feed on by transmitting virus diseases by injecting infected sap from one plant into another.

IDENTIFICATION

Aphids are well known pests, greenfly and blackfly are the commonest ones. Some species attack the roots rather than the leaves. Sticky foliage is caused by the honeydew excreted by the aphids—with a black mould.

Chemical control with contact insecticide for aphids. Systemic insecticide will be more effective on ornamental plants.
Green controls include insecticidal soaps and pirimicarb.

Leaf hoppers are usually green or yellow insects which leap when disturbed.
Chemical control with most contact and systemic insecticides.

Red spider mites are tiny creatures. Their silky webs and pale mottling on the upper surface of leaves are an indication of the pests presence.
Chemical control with a contact insecticide.
Green control is achieved with the predatory mite *Phytoseiulus persimilis* and high humidity.

Scale insects are immobile and scale-like in appearance, usually yellow, brown, dark grey or white.
Chemical control with a contact insecticide for scale.

Thrips are narrow brownish-black insects. Affected leaves have a silvery-white discolouration on the upper surface.
Chemical control with a systemic insecticide.
Green control is best with relatively harmless insecticides such as those based on pyrethrum, sprayed frequently.

Whitefly look like tiny white moths which rise up in a cloud when disturbed.
Chemical control with any contact insecticide for whitefly but spray frequently.
Green control is with a parasitic wasp, *Encarsia formosa*, but only in a greenhouse.

CHEMICAL CONTROL

Leaf-sucking insects hide on the undersides of leaves, so spray both sides of the leaves.

BIOLOGICAL CONTROL

Encarsia formosa is a parasitic wasp that helps to control whitefly. Hang the pack on the plants you want to protect, emerging parasites will feed and start to breed.

| Blackfly | Whitefly | Red spider mite | Leaf hopper | Scale |

PEST CONTROL 2:
LEAF- EATERS

Leaf-eating pests destroy plants, identifying the culprit is not always simple unless they are caterpillars.

IDENTIFICATION

Caterpillars come in various sizes and shapes.
Chemical control with derris dust or other suitable contact insecticide.

CHEMICAL CONTROL

Slug pellets are effective at controlling slugs and snails. Most are coloured blue to discourage birds. To protect pets eating the bait, place bait in a piece of narrow pipe.

Green controls include picking off by hand and spraying with *Bacillus thuringiensis*.

Earwigs are yellowish-brown insects with curved pincers at the rear.
Chemical control with insecticidal powders dusted at the base of plants at dusk.
Green control by making a trap of a pot filled with straw, on top of a cane where the insects gather during the day. Empty regularly.

Slugs and snails are so well-known that they need no description. They either make holes or eat all the leaves. Their slime trails show their route.
Chemical control with slug pellets.
Green control involves making or buying beer traps so that the pests drown in a state of intoxication. Coarse grit sprinkled around crowns and new shoots in spring, will help protect them.

Weevils eat irregularly shaped holes around the edges of leaves. The mature insects are usually grey or black with a short snout and elbowed antennae.
Chemical control by spraying with an insecticide for the pest.
Green control by biological control is under development.

BIOLOGICAL CONTROL

Many kinds of caterpillars can be controlled by a bacterium that causes disease in the insects. If you spray the food plants of the pest species (such as cabbages) you should not upset the health of decorative butterflies that feed on weeds.

Mix up the spray according to instructions supplied and spray before the problem has become a major one.

Caterpillar damage   Snail damage   Earwig damage   Slug damage   Weevils

PEST CONTROL 3: ROOT-EATERS

Root pests often go unnoticed until the plants collapse, but control is possible if you are vigilant.

IDENTIFICATION

Cutworms and leatherjackets Cutworms are caterpillars of moths, and have a caterpillar shape. They are usually brown and live in the soil. The base of the stem is usually gnawed, the plant slowly dies.

Leatherjackets are the larvae of daddy-long-legs, or crane flies, and have tubular bodies.
Chemical control by treating the affected plants with a soil insecticide as soon as damage is seen.
Green control consists of winter digging to expose the grubs to birds, and picking the pests off by hand.

Root flies are numerous, affecting carrots and onions but also bulbs. There are many different species and it is the larvae eating the roots which cause the damage.
Chemical control is difficult and impossible once the grubs are in the roots. Use a soil insecticide when planting vulnerable bulbs and seeds.
Green control consists of firming the soil around roots when planting or thinning. Carrot fly can be deterred by placing a polythene barrier around the plants 45cm (18in) high — this works as the pests fly close to the ground.

Weevils It is the grubs which damage the plant roots. If you find small curved white grubs with brown heads and no legs on the remains of the roots, these are likely to be weevil grubs.
Chemical control is difficult, and soil insecticides have little effect.
Green control is possible with a nematode, which affects the grubs, this is not widely available yet.

CHEMICAL CONTROL

Use recommended soil pest products, either in powder or spray formula for affected areas.

Root fly larvae

Root fly damage

Grubs of weevils

DISEASE CONTROL 1: LEAF DISEASES

Fungus diseases affect the leaves of many plants so grow disease resistant varieties. Spray or remove affected leaves immediately.

Downy mildew

IDENTIFICATION

Downy mildew looks like fluffy white growth on the surface of the leaf. Brown or yellow blotches may be seen on the top surface.
Chemical control by removing affected leaves, spraying plant with a fungicide for downy mildew. Powdery mildew treatments will not be effective for this disease.
Green control consists of removing affected leaves, improving ventilation and plant space.

Leaf spots affect many plants, rose black spot is just one kind. The spots are usually black, brown or yellow.
Chemical control is best achieved by a systemic fungicide — not on edible crops.
Green control by destroying affected leaves promptly.

Powdery mildew looks like a white powdery deposit most commonly found on the upper surface of leaves.
Chemical and green control are as for downy mildew with a wider choice of chemicals.

Leaf spot

Powdery mildew

Rust

Rusts vary in appearance, but most cause yellowish patches on the upper surface of leaves and small brown or orange patches on the reverse sides.
Chemical control with a fungicide for rust. Remove affected leaves to control spread of disease.
Green control is best achieved by removing all affected leaves, improving spacing of plants and increasing ventilation.

CHEMICAL CONTROL

Roses prone to fungus diseases are best sprayed on a regular basis with a systemic fungicide.

DISEASE CONTROL 2: ROOT DISEASES

Most root diseases are of a minor nature, but club root is a serious problem that restricts the types of plants you can grow.

IDENTIFICATION

Blackleg affects cuttings. The base turns black, shrinks, softens and eventually dies.
Chemical control is impossible once blacklegs takes hold but use of a hormone rooting powder at planting may prevent an attack.
Green control is impossible.

Club-root affects members of the Cruciferae family, especially brassicas and wallflowers. The roots swell and growth is very stunted.
Chemical control is difficult as the disease remains in the soil for years. Use a club-root dip when planting.
Green control is best achieved by growing plants in sterilized compost

Foot and root rots affect a number of plants such as peas, beans tomatoes, cucumbers and bedding petunias. The roots turn black and the base of the stems rot.
Chemical control is not practical.
Green control is the most affective: raise plants in sterilized compost, avoid repeat plantings in the same area each year, and destroy diseased plants.

Storage rots affect bulbs and corms in storage, as well as stored onions. Soft patches appear with fungal growth on the surface.
Chemical control by dusting non-edible bulbs, tubers and corms with a fungicide before storing.
Green control is effective. Make sure that the bulbs are dry before storing them, and keep in a cool but frost-free, airy place. Check every few weeks for any soft bulbs and remove and destroy any found.

CHEMICAL CONTROL

Non-edible bulbs, corms and tubers should be dusted with a fungicide before storing to prevent rot.

BIOLOGICAL CONTROL

Bulbs, corms and tubers should be hung up in netting where air can circulate freely.

Blackleg

PHYSIOLOGICAL AND OTHER PROBLEMS

Some problems which appear to be caused by pests or disease have a physiological cause, such as wind chill or sun scorch. Others are caused accidentally by weedkillers, or deficiencies in the soil.

IDENTIFICATION

Cold damage is most on evergreens that are not completely hardy. Leaves are blackened or brown, puckered or withered. Prune out the damaged areas and many plants will outgrow limited damage.

Iron and manganese deficiencies are likely on chalky soils. Symptoms are similar: yellowing leaves, especially at the edges. Apply sequestered iron or trace elements for high soil pH in a chelated formulation.

Fasciated stems can be caused by injury or genetic quirk. The stems are flattened and appear fused together.

Nitrogen deficiency shows itself in pale green leaves which are sometimes mottled or yellowed. Growth is slow. Feed with high-nitrogen fertilizer.

Potassium deficiency shows itself in prematurely autumnal leaves. The leaves may roll inwards. Apply a sulphate of potash or fertilizer high in potassium.

Sun scorch happens behind unshaded glass in a greenhouse or where the temperature is very high. Brown patches on the upper surface of the leaves is the first indication, the edges may brown and become brittle. Improve shading for the plant in hot weather, and improve ventilation.

Weedkiller damage depends on the type of weedkiller used. Selective hormone weedkillers for lawn use will cause distorted growth if they drift onto ornamental plants. Contact weedkillers usually cause pale or bleached areas on foliage. There is nothing you can do except be more careful.

Viruses come in many forms, causing different symptoms. The leaves have a mottled pattern, yellowish stripes, and the plant is stunted. Not all viruses are regarded as undesirable — some striped flowers and variegated leaves, caused by virus infections, are considered attractive. Generally, all plants affected by a virus should be pulled up and destroyed as soon as possible.

Cold damage

Manganese deficiency

Iron deficiency

Nitrogen deficiency

Sun scorch

Virus infection

Fasciated stem

SOWING IN POTS AND TRAYS

Tender bedding plants must be started off indoors or in the greenhouse. Sow in trays if you need a lot of plants, or in pots to save space. Many hardy plants such as rock plants and hardy border perennials can be sown in pots and trays, but they can be put out in cold frames to germinate.

SOWING IN POTS

1 For border perennials, rock plants, house plants and shrubs, sow in pots. Use a rounded presser to firm compost.

2 Sprinkle seeds evenly, using the sand technique if seed is very fine. Stand pot in a bowl of water to moisten the compost, then remove and let it drain.

3 Insert a label then cover with glass or put pot in a propagator if warmth is needed for germination.

4 Alpines and shrubs don't need much warmth so put them in a cold frame. Plunging the pots in sand reduces the risk of the compost drying out.

SOWING FINE SEED

1 If the seed is fine and difficult to handle, mix it with a small amount of silver sand to make spreading easier.

2 Sprinkle the mixture between your finger and thumb, as if sprinkling salt over your food.

SOWING IN TRAYS

1 Fill the tray loosely with sterilized seed compost. Level with the rim, then press down with a piece of wood. Leave a gap of 12mm (0.5in) below the rim. Water the tray before sowing or the seeds will be washed away.

2 Sprinkle seeds thinly over the surface. Large seeds can be spaced individually. Medium-sized seeds can be put in a folded piece of paper, then tap it with a finger to disperse seeds.

3 Sift more compost over the top, if instructions say you should do so.

4 To keep the compost moist either place in a sealed plastic bag or cover with glass.

5 Each day, turn the glass over, or the bag inside out, to reduce condensation drips.

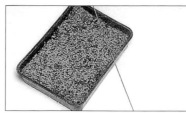

6 Once the seeds germinate, remove the glass or bag. Covering the seeds for too long could encourage disease through high humidity.

PRICKING OUT

Gardening Basics

As soon as seedlings are large enough to handle, prick them out into pots or trays of potting compost to give the seedlings enough space to grow healthily.

PRICKING OUT INTO TRAYS

1 Fill tray with sterilized compost. Level and firm the compost to 12mm (0.5in) below the rim.

2 Use a dibber to loosen the compost and lift out each seedling with as much compost as possible attached.

3 Use a dibber to make a hole deep enough to take the roots. Hold the seedling by a seed leaf. Firm compost gently around roots. Space seedlings 2–5cm (1–2in) apart.

4 Water thoroughly after transplanting and shade from direct sunlight for a couple of days.

PRICKING OUT INTO MODULES

Using pre-formed trays or modules will ensure even spacing of seedlings.

48

TRANSPLANTATION INTO POTS

1 Some plants such as cyclamen, tomatoes and dahlias are best pricked out into individual pots, instead of trays. This gives them more space to grow. Place them in small 8–10cm (3–4in) pots.

2 Once watered, keep the pots out of direct sunlight for a couple of days. Square pots are space saving.

PLUGS AND POT-READY PLANTS

1 Seedlings are often sold in 'plugs', separate blocks of compost. It is possible to do this yourself using trays made for this purpose. Sow one or two seeds in each cell and thin if necessary.

2 Transfer the seedlings into pots or trays as normal. Young plants are sometimes sold by nurseries in larger plugs, these should be potted up separately.

Sowing in cells saves time pricking out. This is suitable for most bedding plants and many vegetables that are started off in the greenhouse.

BORECOLE DWARF GREEN CURLED H

SOWING HARDY ANNUALS

Hardy annuals are undemanding plants that can be sown directly into the ground. Thin them out and water well in dry weather and you will produce masses of flowers with little effort.

SOWING IN ROWS

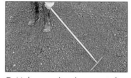

1 Make sure that the area is free of weeds and large lumps of earth, then rake level. Fine soil is needed to germinate seeds.

2 Mark out with sand or grit the areas in which each annual is to grow.

3 Make shallow drills in the soil according to the instructions, and plant in alternate directions to soften the effect.

4 Sow seeds as evenly as possible along the drill. Large seeds can be sown individually.

5 Label each section, rake the soil to cover the seeds.

6 Water well until seeds germinate and are established.

Hardy annuals are the easiest of all flowers to grow. They can be sown where they will flower, bloom quickly, and are usually bright and cheerful. These are godetias.

SOWING BROADCAST

1 Packets of mixed annuals and groups of one type can be sown broadcast (scattered randomly). At the seedling stage it is difficult to tell weeds from annuals. Scatter as evenly as possible.

2 Rake the seeds in to distribute and bury them, raking in different directions.

THINNING

Thin seedlings while young to prevent overcrowding. Hold down the soil on either side of the plant you want to keep, whilst pulling out unwanted plants. Space seedlings at distances recommended on the packet. Water after thinning it weather is dry.

SOWING ALPINES AND SHRUBS

G A R D E N I N G   B A S I C S

Alpine, tree and shrub seeds often need to undergo a period of cold weather. Many prefer to be sown in the autumn and overwintered in a cold frame.

SOWING SLOW-GERMINATING PERENNIALS

1 Fill a small pot with a loam-based seed compost and firm gently.

2 Sow the seed thickly as germination is poor, but do not let the seeds touch each other.

3 Cover the seeds with potting compost, then sprinkle grit or coarse sand over the surface to discourage algae growth.

4 Plunge the pots up to their rims in a cold frame to prevent moisture loss. Cover with a sheet of glass if mice are attracted to the seeds.

PRICKING OUT

Label the pots. Keep the pots watered. Seedlings will usually germinate in the spring and during the summer. Prick them out and grow on in pots or in rows in a nursery bed (see opposite).

Left Aubretias are particularly easy alpines to raise from seed, and they flower quickly. They do not always grow true to type from seed.

BIENNIALS AND PERENNIALS

1 An easy way to raise biennials and border perennials is to sow them in a seed bed in late spring or early summer.

2 Take out shallow drills in rows about 23cm (9in) apart and sow seeds thinly. Water gently, then rake soil over the seeds.

3 Thin the seedlings out, if necessary and plant in another area where they can grow on until the autumn. Rake in garden fertilizer.

4 Space seedlings 15–23cm (6–9in) apart to allow room for growth. Water well.

5 Wallflowers need the growing tip removed every few weeks after transplanting, to encourage bushier plants. Put biennials in their flowering position in the autumn. Leave border perennials until the following spring.

SOFTWOOD AND GREENWOOD CUTTINGS

Softwood and greenwood cuttings root quickly and can be taken from fuchsias and pelargoniums. Greenwood cuttings come from the soft tip of the stem after the first spurt of growth has slowed down.

KEEPING CUTTING FRESH

Softwood cuttings soon wilt, so put them in a polythene bag until they are to be used.

TAKING SOFTWOOD CUTTINGS

1 Many shrubs and pelargoniums (geraniums) can be propagated from soft new shoots. Do not cut below the third leaf from the tip.

2 Trim off the lowest pair of leaves. Trim the base of the stem, cutting straight across the stem just below a leaf joint.

3 Dip the cut tip of each cutting into rooting powder containing a fungicide.

4 Use a dibber to make a hole in a pot of compost for the cutting.

5 Either insert the cuttings around the edges of the pot or put into individual pots. Once watered, place in a humid propagator (or cover with polythene), keep in a warm light place out of direct sunlight.

GARDENING BASICS

TAKING GREENWOOD CUTTINGS

1 Take cuttings once the new growth has slowed down in early summer. For most shrubs, a 10cm (4in) long cutting from the shoot is adequate.

2 Place cuttings in a polythene bag or bowl of water to prevent wilting.

3 Shorten the length of each cutting to 8cm (3in), cutting straight across the stem.

4 Trim leaves from the bottom half of the cutting, using a sharp knife.

5 Dip the cut ends into a rooting hormone to speed up the rooting process.

6 Insert cuttings around the edge of a pot, water with fungicide and allow to drain.

7 Place pot in a warm, humid propagator in light but out of direct sunlight. A polythene bag could be used as an alternative.

GARDENING BASICS

BASAL STEM CUTTINGS

Basal stem cuttings can be taken in spring from many herbaceous plants that produce new shoots at soil level. This method is good for propagating dahlias.

TAKING DELPHINIUM CUTTINGS

1 Use the basal shoots of delphiniums and lupins to make new plants. Remove shoots when they are 8–10cm (3–4in) long.

2 Trim the cuttings with a sharp knife across the end, remove any low leaves. Dip the ends into a rooting hormone.

3 Insert cuttings, one to a pot or two or three around the edge of a pot, into a mixture of peat and sand or a rooting compost. Cover cuttings to provide a humid atmosphere.

Chrysanthemum

TAKING DAHLIA CUTTINGS

1 In late winter place tubers in boxes packing moist compost or peat around them. Keep in a warm light place.

2 When the shoots have grown to about 8cm (3in) long, cut them off close to the tuber.

3 Remove the lowest leaves from the cuttings, and trim straight across just below a leaf joint with a sharp knife.

4 Dip the cut ends into a rooting hormone and insert several cuttings into each pot. Keep moist and pot up when they have rooted.

TAKING CHRYSANTHEMUM CUTTINGS

1 Cut off young shoots about 3–5cm(1–2in) long. Pull off lowest leaves and trim the end with a knife.

2 Insert cuttings around the edge of a pot. They will often root without rooting hormone, but using one will speed up rooting.

3 Cover with an inflated polythene bag. Check regularly, turning the bag to avoid condensation dripping onto leaves. Remove any rotted leaves.

SEMI-RIPE CUTTINGS

Semi-ripe cuttings are a good way to propagate many shrubs. Mid and late summer are the ideal time to take them. Cuttings will form roots in a month or two.

TAKING SEMI-RIPE CUTTINGS

1 Take cuttings of 5–10cm (2–4in) long from shoots that are nearly fully grown. The tip may be soft but the wood at the base should be hardening.

2 Strip the lower leaves from each cutting them trim the length if necessary.

3 Dip the cut end into rooting hormone.

4 Semi-ripe cuttings taken in summer will root in open ground if well watered, but will do better in a cold frame.

5 Firm cuttings to remove air pockets that could cause the cuttings or new roots to dry out.

6 Water with a fungicide added to prevent rot. Water often in dry weather.

7 Label each row to identify cuttings if you take several at the same time.

SOME SHRUBS TO PROPAGATE

The following shrubs root easily from semi-ripe cuttings. There are many others, so be prepared to experiment if your favourite shrub is not in this listing.

Abelia
Buddleia (butterfly bush)
Camelia
Ceanothus (Californian lilac)
Chaenomeles (quince)
Choisya (Mexican orange blossom)
Cistus (sun rose)
Cotoneaster
Daphne
Deutzia
Elaegnus
Escallonia
Euonymus
Forsythia
Fuchsia
Griselinia
Hebe
Helianthemum (rock rose)
Hibiscus
Hydrangea
Ligustrum (privet)
Philadelphus (mock orange)
Pieris
Potentilla
Pyracantha (firethorn)
Rhododendron
Ribes (flowering currant)
Rose
Rosemary
Santolina (cotton lavender)
Syringa (lilac)
Viburnum
Weigela

Santolina

Euonymus

Weigela

SPECIAL CUTTINGS

Some shrubs, such as clematis, sometimes root better if you use special techniques.

INTERNODAL CLEMATIS CUTTINGS

1 Take internodal cuttings to raise a lot of clematis, rather than layering which produces a smaller number of plants.

2 Make cuttings by severing them from the stem *between* leaf joints. Leave 2–5cm (1–2in) of stem below the leaves, with a short stem above leaf joint.

3 Remove one of the leaves, leaving a short stump. Leave the other leaf as a 'handle'.

4 Insert in the compost in the usual way. Pot up the rooted plants individually and grow on for a season before planting out.

HEEL CUTTINGS

1 Some shrubs root better if the cutting is taken with a 'heel' of old wood— a slither of bark.

2 Remove the cutting by pulling downwards so that a piece of stem bark comes away with the cutting.

3 Trim the cutting and insert into compost as usual.

4 Insert cutting, as usual, and put pot in a cold frame or cover with a polythene bag.

Right Juniperus cuttings usually root better if taken with a heel. Make them in early autumn.

Above Cuttings are one of the ways that azaleas can be propagated, they can be taken with or without a heel.

Left Evergreen elaeagnus root easily from cuttings taken in late summer or early autumn. A cutting with a heel can help rooting.

HARDWOOD CUTTINGS

Take hardwood cuttings in late autumn or when shrubs are dormant. Most are easy to root and need less looking after, than other cuttings, as they are left in the ground.

TAKING SEMI-RIPE CUTTINGS

1 Choose shoots grown in the summer, which are firm. Avoid weak and old shoots. Cut off shoots with secateurs, these can be divided up into shorter lengths later.

2 Pull off any dying leaves that remain on the shoot, then cut into sections about 15–23cm (6–9in) long.

3 So that you remember which end is the top, make a sloping cut above the top bud and a horizontal one underneath.

4 Choose a sheltered but not dry part of the garden and make a V-shaped slit trench.

5 To stop water from rotting the base of the cuttings, sprinkle grit or coarse sand along the base of the trench.

SINGLE STEM CUTTINGS

If you are taking cuttings of trees or fruit bushes that you want to grow with a single stem, insert the cutting so the tip is just covered.

6 Insert cuttings vertically 10cm (4in) apart, with only 2–5cm (1–2in) above ground.

Cornus alba and its varieties are grown mainly for their attractive coloured winter stems. They are very easy to propagate from hardwood cuttings.

ROOTING HORMONES

Rooting hormones—which can be powders or liquids—are most useful for plants that are difficult to root. They can be used on all stem cuttings. They are not intended for use on leaf or root cuttings.

Most of the hormones will be taken up through the cut base of the cutting, not through the bark or stem, so only dip the cut surface into the powder or liquid.

If using a powder, dip the tip of the cutting into water first so that the powder adheres to the cutting easily.

Rooting hormones can be formed from different chemicals, suited to hardwood or softwood—most sold to amateurs are all-purpose.

Many contain fungicide, which reduces the risk of rot.

Most rooting hormones used by amateurs come as powders.

Some hormones are dissolved in water or solvents, but those sold to amateurs are usually in gel form.

PLANTS TO TRY

Most deciduous (leaf-shedding) shrubs can be propagated from hardwood cuttings. Popular ones include:

Cotoneaster
Dogwood (*Cornus alba*)
Flowering currant (*Ribes sanguineum*)
Rose (below)
Winter-flowering viburnum

Poplar and willow trees root readily from cuttings.

LAYERING

Layering is an ideal way to propagate shrubs and some house plants. You will usually have a larger plant than from cuttings. Air layering is a good technique if you have a leggy plant bare at the base. Simple layering is best for shrubs in the garden, serpentine layering is good for clematis or honeysuckle.

SIMPLE LAYERING

1 Choose a young, low-growing branch which be bent down easily. Trim leaves and sideshoots off the branch where it meets the soil.

2 Make a hole 10–15cm (4–6in) deep sloping towards the patent plant.

3 Hold the stem in contact with the soil using a peg of bent wire. Ensure that the end of the stem lies vertically against the back of the hole.

4 Return the excavated soil to bury the stem and firm well.

AFTERCARE

• Water thoroughly and prevent soil drying before the plant has rooted.
• Sever the stem from its parent in autumn or spring.
• After severing, pinch out the growing tip to get a bushy plant.
• Lift and replant if well-rooted; if not leave for a year.

PLANTS TO TRY

Most shrubs and some trees can be layered if there are suitable low-growing shoots, these include:
  Corylus avellana 'Contorta'
  Hamamelis (witch hazel)
  Magnolia x soulangeana
  Magnolia stellata
  Rhododendron (opposite)
  Syringa vulgaris (lilac)
  Viburnum

AIR LAYERING

1 Trim off any leaves growing where you want to make a layer. Make a polythene sleeve to go around the stem. Secure the bottom of the sleeve using tape or plastic covered wire.

2 Holding out the sleeve out of the way, use a sharp knife to make a slanting upward cut, half-way through, about 2.5cm (1in) long.

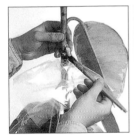

3 Brush a little hormone rooting powder or liquid into the cut, pack with sphagnum moss to keep cut open.

4 Pull the sleeve over the cut area and pack it with moist sphagnum moss. Tie at the top with more tape or wire.

AFTERCARE

- Care for the parent plant normally, do not remove the layered section until you can see roots.
- Once plenty of roots have formed, cut through the stem below the layered area. Tease out some roots when you pot it up.

PLANTS TO TRY

Air layering is commonly used for leggy indoor plants,but it can be used for garden trees or shrubs.
Indoors
Ficus elastica (rubber plant)
Dracaena
Outdoors
Hamamelis (witch hazel)
Magnolia
Rhododendron (below)
Syringa (lilac)

SERPENTINE LAYERING

Strip the leaves from a healthy shoot at points where the stem will be buried, leaving several intact. Make a slanting cut at each joint almost half-way through. Insert a piece of matchstick into the cut to keep it open. Pin down with wire, cover with soil, keep moist.

Plants to try Serpentine layering is suitable for climbers and trailers with long stems that can be pegged down into the ground such as:
Clematis (opposite)
Lonicera (honeysuckle)
Parthenocissus (Boston ivy)

LEAF CUTTINGS

Leaf cuttings can be fun to root, and are ideal for propagating house-plants such as African voilets (*Saintpaulia*) and Cape primroses (*Streptocarpus*).

LEAF PETIOLE CUTTINGS

1 African violets can be propagated from leaf cuttings taken with the stalk (petiole) attached. Choose young healthy leaves.

2 Trim the stalk, insert into a pot of cuttings compost, vermiculite or perlite, so the leaf blade just touches the compost.

4 Keep the compost damp but not wet. Remove condensation. Pot up the plantlet as soon as it is growing well.

3 Cover with the top half of a plastic drinks bottle or an inflated plastic bag. Label and keep in a warm light place.

LEAF SECTION CUTTINGS

1 Cape primrose leaves can be cut into sections 5–8cm (2–3in) wide, with a sharp knife.

2 Push cut section vertically into a tray of compost. Keep the side nearest the leaf stalk downwards, bury one-third of cutting.

3 Keep compost moist and warm, out of direct sunlight. Pot up plantlets individually

African violets are particularly easy to root from leaf cuttings (see leaf petiole cuttings).

LEAF BLADE CUTTINGS

1 *Begonia rex* produce new plants from the leaf blade (lamina). Mature leaves should be used, keeping part of the stem. Cut across the main veins underneath.

2 Place leaf on a tray of compost, pushing the stalk in helps hold the leaf in place. Use a piece of bent wire to hold the veins down onto the compost.

3 It is also possible to hold down the leaf with small-stones.

4 Label, keep tray in a warm place. When small plants develop, separate them carefully and pot up individually.

DIVISION

Division is one of the easiest and quickest methods of propagation. Herbaceous plants benefit from division once they have formed a mature clump of growth.

DIVIDING HERBACEOUS PLANTS

1 Divide large clumps as the shoots emerge in spring using a fork to lift the clump.

2 Use two forks back to back to divide the clump into smaller pieces.

3 Replant without further division unless you wish to have smaller plants. To make smaller plants pull or cut the clump apart. Remove any dead plant material.

4 Rake in a garden fertilizer before replanting the smaller pieces into prepared ground.

DIVIDING FLAG IRISES

1 Divide rhizomatous flag irises after flowering, by lifting with a fork and shaking off the soil.

2 Replant the current season's growth, discard the old part of the rhizome.

3 Trim the leaves to 5–8cm (2–3in) to reduce the water loss whilst new roots grow.

DIVIDING AQUATIC PLANTS

1 To remove the plant from a basket, cut roots flush. Using a spade divide the clump into smaller pieces.

2 Aquatic rushes and irises have very tough roots and a sharp knife may be needed to cut through them. Replant the pieces in fresh compost, placing a new liner in the basket if it is to be re-used.

DIVIDING BEGONIA TUBERS

1 Start off tubers in late winter or early spring, in trays of compost. When shoots can be seen, cut tubers into pieces each one having a shoot or bud.

2 Dust the cut surfaces with fungicide, then pot up individually in small pots.

DIVIDING DAHLIA TUBERS

Division is a good way to produce only two or three extra plants. Divide the tubers in late spring with a sharp knife. Each piece should have buds or new shoots growing and a piece of old stem. Another method starts the tubers off in boxes or trays. When the growth is a few centimetres high, cut through the tuber, making sure that each piece has a shoot. Dust cut surfaces with a fungicide then pot up. Replant outside when the weather if good.

4 Replant spreading the roots either side. Cover the roots with soil, leave the top of the rhizome exposed.

ROOT CUTTINGS

Root cuttings are usually taken in winter when there is not much outdoor propagation to be done. Border plants and alpines root readily with this method.

DIVIDING HERBACEOUS PLANTS

1 Lift the parent plant with a fork to expose the roots.

2 If the plant has fleshy, thick roots cut some off close to the main stem or root.

3 Cut each root, into 5cm (2in) pieces, cutting horizontally across the top and with a sloping cut at the bottom.

4 Insert the cuttings into pots of gritty compost. The top of the cuttings should be flush with the top of the compost.

5 Sprinkle a thin layer of grit over the surface, label and keep in a cold frame or cool greenhouse.

6 Plants with finer roots should be cut into 5–8cm (2–3in) lengths.

7 Lay the cuttings flat on the compost in a tray, cover with compost and store as above.

PLANTS TO TRY

Take root cuttings when the plant is dormant—preferably in early winter.

Perennials to try include acanthus, echinops, gaillardias and border phlox.

Some alpines as well as a few trees, can be raised from root cuttings

Romneya coulteri is an imposing shrub with flowers about 10cm (4in) across on a plant 1.2–1.8m (4–6ft) tall. It can be propagated from root cuttings taken in mid winter, about 7.5cm (3in) in length.

PRUNING 1

Most shrubs require minimal pruning to remove dead or diseased shoots. Some established shrubs benefit from pruning as it can encourage better-flowering or more compact plants

PRUNING FOR COLOURED STEMS

1 Shrubs such as the Dogwood need to be pruned annually or every second year to encourage new stems, like these shown here.

2 Prune in early spring cutting back each stem to an outward facing bud 5cm (2in) from the stump of hard wood.

3 Although the pruning looks severe, new shoots will soon appear.

PRUNING GREY-LEAVED SHRUBS

1 Prune small grey-leaved shrubs in early spring to prevent them getting straggly.

2 Cut close to the base, to where new shoots can be seen.

3 After pruning the plant will look like this but new shoots will soon grow to form a compact shrub.

PRUNING THE WHITEWASH BRAMBLE

1 This shrub is grown for its decorative winter stems that arise directly from the ground. Prune these annually in late winter or early spring.

2 Pruning is simple. Cut off all stems close to the ground, wearing gloves for protection.

3 New shoots grow quickly and these will be more attractive than the old canes.

PRUNING HEATHERS

1 Prune heathers by clipping them with shears to keep them compact and neat.

2 Trim the shoots back after flowering. Prune winter-flowering heathers in spring taking care not to cut into old wood.

Heathers become woody with age. Keep them in shape by clipping the dead heads off after flowering.

PRUNING 2

Shrubs such as buddleias need pruning every year and brooms benefit too from pruning. Cistus don't need routine pruning, but growth will be stimulated and more flowers produced if it is pruned.

PRUNING DECIDUOUS SUCKERING SHRUBS

Shrubs such as *Kerria japonica* and *Leycesteria formosa* will be improved by pruning every spring. Prune the flowered stems back to half their original length, to where there is a new shoot after flowering.

Remove about one-third of all stems to within 5–8cm (2–3in) of the ground. Cut back hard any diseased, damaged, or weak shoots.

PRUNING TO A FRAMEWORK

1 Plants that flowered the previous year on shoots produced that year need pruning every spring to keep them compact.

2 Cut back all shoots in spring to within two buds of the previous year's growth.

3 Although the pruning seems harsh, new shoots will grow rapidly and flower later.

REDUCING NEW GROWTH BY HALF

1 Shrubs such as broom and genista, will flower well without pruning but become straggly, with a bare base. Pruning to keep the plants compact is best done when the plant is young.

2 Prune back all green shoots by half the length of the light green growth. Do not cut back old, dark wood.

PRUNING SLOW-GROWING SUMMER-FLOWERING SHRUBS

1 Slow-growing shrubs that flower on sideshoots produced the previous year, grow well without pruning. You can keep them shapely and stimulate more sideshoots by pruning after flowering has finished.

2 Cut back the new growth— which is soft and pale—by about two-thirds, cutting to a leaf joint or a new shoot.

Climbers need careful pruning to restrict their height and spread, and to keep them flowering well towards the base.

PRUNING A RAMBLER ROSE

1 Cut out any very old, dead or diseased shoots to the base using long-handled pruners, after flowering.

2 Prune each main shoot of all sideshoots to between two and four pairs of leaves from the main stem.

PRUNING A CLIMBING ROSE

1 Cut out any dead shoots and one or two very old main stems can be cut to the base.

2 Grow new shoots by cutting one or two thick shoots back to 30cm (12in).

3 Reduce the length of all sideshoots to about 15cm (6in).

PRUNING CLEMATIS

1 If your clematis flowers from mid or late summer, prune severely in late winter or early spring, before new growth commences.

2 New shoots produced will flower later in the year.

3 If your clematis flowers in early to mid summer, you must prune more selectively. Before new growth begins, cut back about a third of the stems to about 30cm (12in) above ground.

4 To restrict the plant size and grow new sideshoots, prune back the remaining long branches to a pair of strong buds.

5 If your clematis has small blooms and flowers in spring or early summer, prune only to restrict size, after flowering.

Right Most clematis that flower on old wood require minimal pruning. Those that flower on current growth will become bare of flowers at the base unless pruned annually.

RUSTIC ARCHES AND PERGOLAS

An arch or pergola made from rustic timber is fairly simple to construct and looks good with climbing plants. The bark can be left on or if stripped, the wood will be easier to work with.

Rustic poles can be used to make an attractive support for climbing plants. The same basic joints are used.

A RUSTIC PERGOLA

1 A pergola should be first be planned on paper to ensure it suits the size of your garden.

2 The simplest way to fix horizontal poles to the uprights is to make a notch in the top of each upright, to fit the horizontal pole.

3 For a long pergola, saw two opposing and matching notches as shown. The join must occur over an upright pole. Fix with rustproof nails.

4 Notch the cross-pieces with a V-shape first, then adjust with a chisel before nailing.

A RUSTIC ARCH

1 Before cutting any timber. sketch your design onto paper. A basic design is shown here but it can be modified to suit your needs. Remember to allow about 60cm (2ft) extra on uprights to sink into the ground.

2 Assemble the pieces to your own design using a series of basic, strong joints.

3 Where two pieces cross, mark the position and cut halving joints in each one.

4 Wood glue, in addition to rustproof nails, can be used to improve joint strength.

Opposite Clematis are often grown against a wall, but are good for arches.

5 Bird's mouth joints are used for joining some of the pieces. Mark the pieces, then cut out a V-shape about 2.5cm (1 in) deep. Saw the other piece to fit and nail diagonally through the joint.

6 Assemble the sides on the ground first, and make the top separately. Hold the uprights in the prepared holes with wooden struts first of all while you drill and then screw the top into position.

FENCES

Every garden has a boundary, and unless it's secure your garden is at risk. Walls and fences do more than just contain people and animals, they can look attractive and provide the vertical spaces needed for your climbing plants.

ERECTING A PANEL FENCE

1 Panel fences are easy to erect if you use post spikes. Just use a special tool to protect the top, then drive into the ground.

2 Spikes must be absolutely vertical, so keep checking with a spirit-level.

3 Once the post spike is in the ground then the post itself can be inserted. Check again that it is vertical.

4 Lay the panel on the ground in position. Mark the next point for a post spike.

5 Drive the spike in, vertically. Do not leave in position or the panel will be difficult to fix.

6 Nail panel brackets to the post already in position, and on to the next post to be erected at the correct height.

7 Insert panel, and while some-one holds it in position erect the next post. Nail through the brackets into the panel.

8 Check the panel is horizon-tal before and after nailing.

9 Finish off the post by nailing a post cap to the top, which prevents water soaking into the timber.

Right There are other fence designs to try. Here, vertical boards have been nailed either side of the horizontal bars, so that they overlap slightly.

WALLS

Tall boundary walls do not make a good DIY project unless you have bricklaying experience. A low garden wall like this one is suitable as an internal divider as well as a low boundary, and makes a simple bricklaying job with which to start.

MORTAR AND CONCRETE MIXES

For foundations for walls, drives or pre-cast paving
1 part cement
2.5 parts sharp sand*
3.5 parts aggregate*
* Instead of using separate aggregate and sand, you can use 5 parts of combined aggregate to every 1 part cement.

Bedding mortar (to bed and joint concrete/brick paving)
1 part cement
5 parts sharp sand

Masonry mortar (for brickwork)
1 part cement
3 parts soft sand

All parts are by volume. In hot climates, setting retardants may be needed; in cold climates, a form of antifreeze may be required.

BUILDING A LOW BRICK WALL

1 All walls need a foundation. Remove a trench 30cm (12in) deep and put in hardcore. Place pegs as a guide for the concrete. Check levels of the pegs.

2 Pour in the concrete, and level off with the pegs. Tamp the concrete level and remove air pockets with a piece of wood.

3 Leave the concrete to harden for a few days, then lay the first course of bricks. It is vital to form a small pier at each end — and at intervals along the wall if it is long — as shown.

4 Continue to lay courses, first laying a ribbon of mortar on top of the previous row, 'buttering' one end of each brick, as shown.

5 Use a spirit level regularly, strike off excess mortar from the sides of the wall as you work.

6 Use the handle of the trowel to firm and adjust the level of each brick as it is laid.

7 Finish off the wall with coping, and pier caps. This makes the wall look better and protects the brickwork from moisture.

Bricks are a 'sympathetic' building material for paths and walls, integrating house and garden. A raised bed like this is a straightforward project to try, even if you have no previous experience.

SURFACES AND PATHS 1

Along with the lawn, hard surfaces such as paving create the backbone of the garden. Plants add the shape and form, but paving has a profound effect on the visual impact of a garden, so it's important to take care to get it looking good.

LAYING PAVING SLABS

1 Try to prepare proper foundations for paths or patios. The depth of hardcore depends on the weight the paving has to support: 5–10cm (2–4in) for foot traffic, 15cm (6in) for vehicles.

2 Compact the ground either by treading it, tamping it or by using a flat-plate vibrator like this, good for a large area. They can easily be hired.

3 Add the hardcore, checking the depth with a steel rule and a straight edge.

4 Compact the hardcore with a sledge-hammer or club, to break down large pieces

5 Bed the slabs with blobs of mortar (1 part cement to 5 parts sharp sand) one in each corner, one in the centre.

6 Position the slab as accurately as possible, and lower it down from one side.

7 Tap it into position with the handle of a mallet or hammer, check levels with a spirit-level. A slight slope is needed for a large area to allow water to drain away.

8 Place the spirit level across other slabs to check all levels are the same.

9 Paving slabs are designed to either fit flush or have mortar joints. Use spacers to make an even gap for mortar.

10 Fill the joints with a small pointing trowel, recessing the mortar slightly.

LAYING BRICK PAVING

1 Here the bricks are shown bedded on mortar, the base is prepared as for paving slabs but an even layer of mortar is spread across the area being laid. Lay the sides first to make it easier to check levels. The bricks can also be laid on sand.

2 Lay several rows of bricks in your pattern, pressing them into the mortar. Tamp down on a piece of wood, to ensure they are level.

3 To mortar the joints brush dry mortar mix into the gaps. Press down with a piece of wood to remove air pockets.

4 Water with a watering can fitted with a fine rose. Do not flood the area. Clean mortar stains with a damp cloth before they dry.

Right Bricks and plants look good together, as these tumbling petunias testify.

SURFACES AND PATHS 2

Paths and other hard surface areas can be the dominant part of the garden design, so mix materials and surfaces together: the stepping-stone path pictured opposite makes an imposing focal point but is practical in that it protects the lawn too.

LAYING PAVERS

1 Clay pavers look like bricks but are thinner and fit together without mortar joints.
After preparing a sub-base of 5–10cm(2–4in) compacted hardcore, mortar in position a firm edge to work from. Check levels and adjust if necessary.

2 Lay a 5cm (2in) bed of sand. Ensure that the pavers will be level with the edging when laid on the sand. Use battens as a height gauge, to enable a third piece of wood to level the sand.

3 As you lay the pavers in the required pattern, check that they butt up against each other and to the edging.

4 Hiring a flat-plate vibrator is the easiest way to settle the pavers into the sand. Tamping over a piece of wood will also be effective.

5 Brush sand over the pavers to fill the joints. Vibrating or tamping the pavers again may require more sand to be brushed into the joints.

LAYING STEPPING STONES

1 Pace out the area to indicate where each stone should be when you walk with a normal stride.

2 Lay the stones on the lawn, stand back to check that they look right visually.

3 Walk over the stones once more before you set them into the lawn, to make sure the spacing is comfortable.

A stepping-stone path can take the eye across to another focal point, protecting the lawn and your shoes.

4 Cut around the edge of each stone with a spade, deep enough to be able to remove a slice of grass, slightly deeper than the stepping-stone.

5 Slice beneath the grass with a spade, then lift out the piece of turf.

6 Use a little sand to level the base and bring the stone to the right height. Check the level and set just below the surrounding grass.

SURFACES AND PATHS 3

A large area of plain paving can look boring so think about creating an interesting effect by mixing materials. Crazy-paving can give a garden an old-fashioned feel especially if you choose natural stone or a sympathetic substitute.

LAYING CRAZY PAVING

1 Always lay the pieces dry first. Lay large pieces with a straight edges first, at the sides. You can fill in with smaller pieces once these are in place.

2 Once the pieces have been arranged loosely, start to bed them on a mortar mix (1 part cement to 5 parts sharp sand).

3 Use a piece of board across the width of the paving and tamp to create a level finish.

MIXING MATERIALS

Do not be afraid to mix materials: railway sleepers and bricks or clay pavers look good together, gravel softens the harshness of rectangular paving slabs, and rows of bricks break up areas of concrete.

4 Finish off by mortaring between the joints, using a small pointing trowel. You can add a cement dye to match the stone colour.

Right
Combining pavers with a range of pebbles creates an unusual surface.

INTRODUCING PEBBLES

1 Beach pebbles can be used to make a paved area more interesting, or to fill in gaps created when you lay a curved path. Create a bed of mortar, then lay the stones as closely as you can.

2 Use a stout piece of wood, laid across the adjoining slabs, to ensure that the tops of the pebbles are flush with the paving. Tap the wood with a hammer to bed them in evenly.

EDGINGS

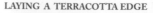

A smart edge will put that finishing touch to a path, bed or border and will prevent wear and tear at the lawn edges.

1 Excavate a shallow trench deep enough to take the edging. The design being laid is the rope pattern.

2 Chisel off any mortar or rubble protruding beneath the path so the edging can be laid flush with the path.

3 Tap each piece down with the handle of a hammer, checking levels visually.

4 Back fill with soil, compact it to stabilize each piece. Add more soil and compact again.

5 Use a long spirit level to ensure that the edging is straight, adjusting height if necessary.

FIXING A WOODEN EDGE

1 Unwind the roll, and cut to size through the strands of wire with pliers or wire-cutters.

2 Dig out a trench at the right depth to allow the edging to sit in place.

3 Join pieces by wiring together in position. Check the level and height, then back fill with soil and compact it.

4 Lay a long piece of wood across the top of the edging, and knock it firmly into place with a club hammer, ensuring the top is level.

GARDENING BASICS

LAYING A LAWN EDGING STRIP

1 Use a spade to form a slit trench along the edge of the lawn, keeping it as vertical as possible.

2 Unroll the strip and cut it to size. Lay it loosely in the trench to estimate the length.

3 Back fill with soil, firming it without pressing so hard that you distort the shape of the edging.

4 Finish off by tapping it level with the handle of a hammer over a piece of wood. Make sure the edging is not above the lawn level, or the mower may be damaged.

A brick edging gives a smart finish to a path or lawn.

FLOWERS & FOLIAGE

No matter how well designed a garden is, with features like patios, pergolas and ponds, it is the flowers and foliage that make a garden such a pleasant place to relax in. In the following pages you will find plenty of advice on how to get the very best from your ornamental plants, as well as how to create features such as ponds, rock gardens and lawns.

Opposite
Be flexible in the way you approach your planting. In this border there is a happy mixture of annuals and shrubby plants together with herbaceous plants.

INTRODUCTION

Flowers and foliage are the flesh that clothes the skeleton of the hard landscaping. They give the garden shape by softening harsh outlines, adding colour and providing plenty of textures.

The plants used and the way they are arranged are a personal choice. Planting 'rules' should only ever be treated as guidelines which you can then interpret to suit your taste and garden layout.

Above Spring would not be spring without daffodils in their many varieties.

If starting from scratch, make sure that the garden framework is right before you begin planting. It is easier to undertake major construction work before the garden is planted. If lots of plants are needed, it is worth propagating your own.

Make the lawns after the hard landscaping, or improve existing grass. Lawns form the largest percentage of ground-cover in most gardens. Getting this area right will have an enormous

Above Use annuals with traditional border plants to create a 'cottage garden' atmosphere.

Left Tubs of colour help to bring life to an otherwise green area. The lavatera in the border is a good choice because it flowers for many months.

Left Few trees or shrubs have a long flowering season, so make the most of foliage. Golden *Sambucus racemosa* contrasts with a purple variety of *Cotinus coggygria*.

Above Hanging baskets add colour and height to a dull spot.

Below Pelargoniums are traditional summer bedding plants.

impact on the overall impression of the garden.

When you plant beds and borders, balance your long-term aims with immediate impact. Plants herbaceous perennials and shrubs first, as they take at least a year to start growing well, and fill in the gaps with plenty of bedding plants and bulbs for instant colour.

Make sure you get the best from your greenhouse, which can become an interesting year-round hobby in itself.

IMPROVING A COLD OR WINDY GARDEN

An exposed or cold garden is problematic. If you choose suitable plants and use shelter belts and windbreaks, you can still enjoy the benefits of a beautiful garden.

PLANTING CONIFERS

Conifers are best bought as small pot-grown plants, which will keep the cost down and species suitable for growing against a wall will soon grow tall.

ARTIFICIAL WINDBREAKS

Moulded plastic windbreak nets will give protection for five to ten years and are useful while hedges and living screens are becoming established. Nail or staple the netting to stout posts 1.8m (6ft) apart.

Plastic webbing lasts for a similar time and is useful for vegetable or fruit gardens where appearance is not so important. Stretch each strand tight, then staple to the posts.

PLANTING A SHELTER BELT

A living shelter belt filters the wind and reduces its velocity, so that the plants are protected.

AVOIDING TURBULENCE

When wind hits a solid object it creates turbulence, which will damage plants.

Hedges and screens of tall shrubs are efficient wind breaks, reducing the wind velocity and turbulence.

1 To improve the soil structure properly, fork in garden compost or manure into a 60cm (2ft) wide strip.

2 Break down any large clumps of earth before planting and sprinkle on fertilizer (use a slow-acting one in winter)

SCREENS AND THICK HEDGES

If you need protection from the wind or sound proofing from traffic, plant a double hedge. Space the plants 60–90cm (2–3ft) apart, in two staggered rows.

If the site is very exposed, a shelter belt of trees will give more protection than a double hedge. Plant trees 1.2–1.8m (4–6ft) apart so they grow into each other.

3 Garden lines ensure that the row of trees will be straight. Plant the trees 30–60cm (1–2ft) apart, staggered if the area is very windy.

4 Hedging plants are sold in bundles of bare-rooted plants. Keep the roots moist until you are ready to plant them out.

AVOID FROST TRAPS

In sloping gardens, placing hedges at the highest level, with an opening at the lowest level lets the cold air flow downhill.

5 Remove the plants one at a time, digging a large hole and spreading out the roots.

6 Always firm the soil well to remove air pockets and to anchor the roots firmly.

7 Rake the soil level, then water thoroughly. Keep well watered for the first season.

FLOWERS & FOLIAGE

PLANTING AND GROWING SHRUBS 1

Shrubs form a permanent framework for the garden, giving it shape over the year. Use them as a border or in mixed borders, as a specimen or a focal point plant. Get them off to a good start and your shrubs will provide years of pleasure in return for the minimum of time and effort.

BALLED PLANTS

1 Some plants are sold with their roots wrapped in hessian or a plastic material. They are usually cheaper than container grown plants of the same size.

2 Prepare the ground as for container-grown plants, checking the depth of the hole as shown.

3 Untie the wrapper when the shrub is in position and at the right depth, sliding it out of the hole. Try not to disturb the ball of soil.

4 Replace the soil, firming it well to remove air pockets and stabilize the shrub.

5 Water thoroughly, then apply a mulch of chipped bark, garden compost to conserve moisture and suppress weeds.

CONTAINER-GROWN SHRUBS

1 Space the potted shrubs out on to the ground to assess their final position in the border. This makes adjustments easier.

2 Dig over the ground, remove weeds, and fork in well-rotted manure or garden compost.

3 Set the plant in the hole in its pot, checking that the new soil level will match the old soil mark on the stem. Use a cane to check the levels.

IMAGINATIVE PLANTING

Shrub borders are often large but a small border can be planted using dwarf shrubs. Choose a mixture of foliage and flowering shrubs, deciduous and evergreen, so there is plenty of interest all year round.

In small gardens a mixed border can be used with tall shrubs at the back and herbaceous plants at the front, with evergreen shrubs for winter interest.

Some shrubs make good focal point plants. Plant them either in containers, as isolated specimens or as a group in a lawn. Use a bright flowering shrub as a focal point to view across

the garden against a background of less colourful shrubs.

Foliage lasts much longer than flowers and in a dull or shady area of the garden,

yellow leaves can be almost as bright as blooms. Group foliage shrubs together for an attractive picture throughout the summer.

PLANTING EVERGREENS

Shield from cold and drying winds until they are rooted into the soil. Make a shelter out of a sheet of polythene fixed to canes.

SPACING SHRUBS

After five to ten years most shrubs will become overcrowded so plant shrubs with final spacings in mind. Fill gaps with cheap, quick-growing shrubs.

1 If roots are tightly wound around the sides of the pot, tease some of them out to encourage them to grow into the surrounding soil quickly.

2 Replace the soil and firm it in well to remove any air pockets that could cause the roots to dry out.

3 If the soil is poor, apply a fertilizer around the plant avoiding the stem. Water well and apply a thick mulch of garden compost or chipped bark.

PLANTING AND GROWING SHRUBS 2

FLOWERS & FOLIAGE

Established shrubs need little routine care, but weeding, feeding and mulching will keep them looking good. If a shrub has been planted in the wrong place, or has outgrown the area, it may be possible to move it to another part of the garden.

MOVING AN ESTABLISHED SHRUB

1 Quite large shrubs can be moved with care. Move deciduous shrubs when they are dormant and evergreens in the autumn or spring.

2 Dig a trench all around the shrub, forking around the roots to loosen them.

3 Use a fork to remove more soil if the shrub is large, being careful not to damage the roots.

4 When the root ball is a manageable size, use a spade to cut underneath it, working around the plant evenly.

5 Make sure the new hole is large enough to take the shrub. Roll up a piece of hessian or plastic sheeting and position against the root ball. Tilt the plant back and push the hessian underneath it, rocking the root ball over it.

6 Tie the hessian around the root ball. Lifting the shrub is likely to need two pairs of hands. Only small shrubs can be lifted easily by one person.

7 Use a barrow or trolley to move the shrub to its new home if necessary. Remove the wrapping material carefully. After filling in the hole and firming, water well and keep watered for several months in dry weather.

WEEDING

1 If annual weeds are a problem, you can use some contact weedkillers if you protect the stems and leaves. Use a dribble bar on the watering can to prevent spray drift.

2 Some weedkillers can be used with care around established shrubs to prevent weed seedlings emerging.

3 Hoeing and hand-weeding works well provided you do not let perennial weeds get established.

4 A mulch of garden compost or chipped bark will control weeds and cover bare soil.

5 Established shrubs do not usually need annual feeding, but young shrubs benefit from a dose of general fertilizer in the spring. If a shrub is not thriving, apply a little fertilizer.

6 Acid-loving shrubs can thrive in alkaline soils if they are treated with a chelated iron twice a year.

PLANTING GROUND-COVER SHRUBS

1 Ground-cover shrubs will suppress weeds after a few years growth. Planting through garden matting is simple and effective. Remove weeds first, then tuck in the edges of the matting into the ground to secure it. This method does not suit all colonizing plants as the matting can suppress the plants as well as the weeds.

2 Cut a cross shape in the sheet to plant shrubs.

3 Plant the shrubs through the slit: a trowel can be used with small plants.

4 The matting will be concealed when the plants grow, but can be covered with chipped bark initially.

PLANTING CLIMBERS AND TRAILERS 1

Climbers need special care as they are often planted in dry areas, in the 'rain shadow' of walls, fences or trees. Take extra care when planting climbers so they get a good start with support to train them.

AIM HIGH

Fix trellis above soil level as shoots need support from about 30cm (12in) or higher. Plan to fix the trellis with the base about 30–45cm (12–18in) above the ground. This will allow more height on which to secure the climber.

PLANTING A CLIMBER

1 Fix the support first. Then dig a large hole to take the root ball, 45cm (18in) away from the wall. Work compost into the base of the hole.

2 Position the plant so that it leans towards the wall at 45° angle, and check the level with surrounding soil with a cane or stick.

3 Tease out a few roots from the root ball, replace and firm the soil. Water well.

4 Untie any shoots fixed to the cane. Tie them to the wall support, spread them out widely, vertically and horizontally, so the plant will not be bare at the base.

FIXING A BOUGHT TRELLIS

1 Expandable wooden trellises are ideal for lightweight plants such as large-flowered clematis, but unsuitable for vigorous climbers or wall shrubs. Expand the trellis to the required size, then mark fixing positions on the wall. Drill and plug the wall, allowing a gap for spacers.

2 Use small scraps of wood to hold the trellis away from the wall. Fix with rustproof screws.

PLASTIC TRELLISES

Plastic-covered metal trellises for clematis and other climbers that are not too vigorous usually come with spacer and fixing screws. If fixing to a brick wall, drill holes with a masonry drill and use a wall plug the correct size.

PLANTING TIPS

Your climber will grow quickly if you add as much compost as you can, before planting. Adding moisture-retaining material is important, as the area used for planting climbers is usually drier than other positions in the garden.

To keep the ground moist, mulch the ground after planting with chipped bark or a similar material. Aim for a 5cm (2in) minimum depth of mulch.

PLANTING A TRAILER

1 Prostrate or low-growing plants will tend to tumble over the edge of a raised bed easier if they are planted at an angle. Set the root ball at an angle of 45°, growing towards the edge of the wall.

2 Trailers such as ground ivy will grow in all directions if not trained. Plant close to the edge of the bed, then direct as many shoots as possible down the front. Pinch out shoots growing inwards.

PLANTING CLIMBERS AND TRAILERS 2

Even if your patio is wall-to-wall paved, there are ways to plant climbers to soften the brickwork, without fixing trellis. Use self-clinging climbers, or support with wires or wall ties.

FIXING WITHOUT A SUPPORT

Lead-headed nails
Useful for fixing small climbers to old walls with soft mortar. Drive them in with a hammer, then fold the soft flap over to hold the shoot.

Epoxy resin ties A plastic tie you 'glue' by mixing a special putty with a hardener and pressing to the wall.

PLANTING IN PAVING

1 Lift one or two paving slabs next to the wall. Chisel away any mortar and remove the sub-base for the paving.

2 Once soil is found, add garden compost and slow-release fertilizer. Fork together, mixing it thoroughly. If the area is small, use a small border fork to mix together.

3 Plant the climber as described in the next section. The soil can be covered with fine gravel or beach pebbles to make it more attractive on a patio.

PLANTING A CLIMBER IN A CONTAINER

1 A container can be sited on top of paving. Use a large container as wall shrubs and climbers need space.

2 Place a layer of rubble or broken clay pots in the base to help water drain freely, then fill with a loam based compost.

3 Plant firmly and water well. Train to the support. Plant small ivies or annual trailers to cascade over the front of the container for summer colour.

SECURING CLIMBERS AND WALL SHRUBS

1 Old walls may have a soft lime-based mortar, so vine eyes (metal tags with a hole through which you can fix a wire) can be knocked in. House mortar will be too hard, so drill and plug the wall before inserting screw-type eyes. Stretch galvanized wire between the eyes 30–45cm (12–18in) apart. Twiners like clematis need vertical wires to form a mesh.

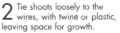

2 Tie shoots loosely to the wires, with twine or plastic, leaving space for growth.

Right
Climbers such as *Lonicera periclymenum,* a honeysuckle, are vigorous climbers quickly covering a wall or fence.

PLANTING TREES 1

Trees should always be planted with care. You have only one chance to get them off to a good start, so choose your tree and a suitable position with care, then plant and stake it carefully.

PLANTING A TREE IN A LAWN

1 Mark out the edge of the circular bed 90cm–1.2m (3–4ft) across. Push the spade in vertically, then at a shallow angle.

2 Remove the top 30cm (12in) of soil, then fork over the rest thoroughly working in compost or manure.

3 Insert the stake before you plant then hammer it in.

4 If planting a container-grown tree, tease out some of the roots before planting.

5 Put the roots in the soil, lay a cane across the hole to check the soil levels.

BARE-ROOTED TREES

Bare-rooted trees should be planted while they are still dormant— between late autumn and early spring. Spread the roots out widely, checking that the soil level on the stem is the same as the surrounding soil.

6 Return the soil and tread in firmly to remove air pockets. If the soil is poor, rake in a slow-release fertilizer.

7 Water well, then apply a mulch at least 5cm (2in) thick to keep down weeds and conserve moisture.

106

HOW TO APPLY A TREE TIE

1 Select a tree tie that has a buffer to separate the stake from the tree itself.

2 Loop the tie around the tree, push the free end through the spacer.

3 Push the end through the tie around the stake. Leave the end long as the tie will need adjusting as the trunk grows.

4 To prevent the tie slipping, nail it in position. Staking is needed only for three or four years.

POPULAR STAKES

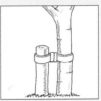

High stakes are best for trees which have long thin stems.
Low stakes suit most trees as they allow the stem to flex in the wind.
Angled stakes are good if adding a stake after the tree has been planted. Insert at an angle to miss the root ball.

Plant a tree in your lawn to suit the size of your garden. Where space is restricted, plant a small conifer.

PLANTING TREES 2

After planting, make sure your trees grow into an attractive shape, reduce competition from weeds and protect them from animals.

WIND PROTECTION

Evergreen trees and shrubs will benefit from wind protection in the first autumn and winter. Fix windbreak netting around canes but leave the top open. Remove in the spring.

FORMATIVE TRAINING

1 If you want a multi-stemmed tree, buy one with shoots along the trunk. Prune only the shoots that cross others or are badly positioned. Do this only once.

2 If you want a tree with a clear trunk, cut back all the shoots above the branching head to 10–15cm (4–6in). When the tree is dormant, cut these back to the stem.

3 If you want a tree with a dominant central leading shoot, prune back all other shoots to the stem leaving the dominant, most upright shoot to continue growing.

4 Some trees are best with a rounded, branching head. Remove lower shoots to make a clear stem. Remove the tip of the leading shoot when the tree has reached its final height.

CONSERVING MOISTURE AND CONTROLLING WEEDS

1 Thorough watering will help the tree to become established more quickly. Insert a pot close to the roots and water will penetrate the roots easier.

2 A mulch will conserve moisture, keep down weeds and look attractive. Lay at least 5cm (2in) depth to be effective.

3 Mulching sheets are not as attractive, but just as effective at controlling weeds and retaining moisture.

USING A TREE GUARD

1 If animals strip off the tree bark in your garden, provide guards for new trees. Those available are only suitable for trees with clear stems. Start at the bottom of the stem and wind the guard around as you work upwards.

2 Wire netting can be used for conifers. Insert four canes around the plant and secure small-wire netting to this. Secure to the canes with galvanised wire.

GROWING BULBS 1

Bulbs, corms and tubers can be used to good effect in borders, in grass, formal beds and the home. Bulbs are available in the spring for summer flowering, so bulb planting is not just for the autumn.

PLANTING IN A BORDER

1 Dig a hole large enough to take a group of bulbs. Fork in compost or manure if the soil is poor.

2 Bulbs suitable for a border need good drainage. Add a layer of grit or coarse sand before planting.

3 Space out the bulbs, planting at a depth which allows twice their own depth of soil.

4 To deter slugs and improve drainage, sprinkle more grit around them.

5 If planting summer-flowering bulbs, mark their position to avoid planting others in the same spot.

Left Crocuses can grow in pots and bowls indoors, window boxes, beds and borders to bring colour when few other plants are flowering. They can even be planted in the lawn.

PLANTING IN GRASS

1 Use an edging iron to cut a straight line into the grass where you want to plant.

2 Use a spade to slice beneath the grass, then fold back the turf for planting.

3 Fork over the compacted ground to loosen it. Add fertilizer at the same time.

4 Bulbs, corms and tubers look best if scattered randomly as this gives a natural effect.

5 Large bulbs need planting with a trowel in twice their own depth of soil. Small bulbs can be pressed into the soil.

6 Fold back the turf flaps and firm carefully. Check the lawn level and adjust with extra soil if necessary.

7 Large bulbs can also be planted with a bulb planter instead of lifting the turf.

8 Most bulb planters are designed to release the core of soil easily.

9 Crumble some soil from the bottom of the core to cover the bulb. Press the plug of grass back into the hole.

GROWING BULBS 2

For indoors in early spring, try growing hyacinths in a glass.

HYACINTHS IN GLASSES

2 Below When the bud is emerging and beginning to show colour, move the bulb to a light, warm place to flower.

1 Above Buy good sized bulbs. Fill the glass with water so that the bulb base is just clear of the water. Keep the glass in a cold, dark place. Top up with water whenever necessary.

PLANTING HYACINTHS IN A BOWL

1 Part fill a bowl with bulb fibre, them put three or five bulbs in place so that a third of the bulb will be visible above the compost.

2 Water, then place the bulbs in a cool, shady place outdoors. Protect the bulbs with a plastic bag then cover with grit, sand or peat.

3 When the shoots reach 2.5–5cm (1–2in) tall, bring them into a light, cool place indoors. When the buds emerge move them to a warm area.

AFTER FLOWERING

1 Never force bulbs into a second year, plant them out in the garden and they may bloom another year. Discard bulbs forced in glasses or on pebbles as they do not do well after this treatment.

2 Let the bulb leaves die down naturally and only cut them off when they begin to wither. Do not bend or tie the leaves as next years flowering could be reduced.

3 Where bulbs grow in a lawn, do not cut the grass for at least six weeks after flowering. Wait until the leaves turn yellow then cut them off with shears before mowing.

DIVIDING BULBS 'IN THE GREEN'

Some bulbs are sold 'in the green', with the leaves on. Lift an overcrowded clump with a fork and separate it. Replant the smaller bulbs where they are, larger bulbs can be moved elsewhere. Water well.

DIVIDING OVER-CROWDED CLUMPS

1 Poor flowering could be caused by overcrowding. Lift, divide and replant the clumps of bulbs. Do this when the plant is dormant, but before the leaves die down completely, so it is easier to see where the clumps are.

2 Separate the clump into smaller pieces and replant some of the larger bulbs in the same way. Discard surplus bulbs or replant elsewhere.

LIFTING AND STORING

1 Some bulbs are best lifted and stored after flowering, to protect them from frost. Use a fork to carefully lift the bulbs. Keep the large bulbs and discard smaller ones. Place the bulbs to be saved on a wire rack for a few days.

2 Shake the bulbs in a bag of fungicide, remove them with care and store in paper bags in a cool dry place.

GROWING HERBACEOUS PLANTS 1

Herbaceous borders are less popular than they used to be, but they can be used in an original and imaginative way, even in small gardens.

PLANTING HERBACEOUS PLANTS

1 Prepare the ground well, adding compost and raking the ground level, before planting. Space the plants out on the ground before planting. Try to visualize the mature size of each plant before finally deciding on the plant positions. Ground-cover plants are best planted in bold groups and perennials in groups of three or five of each plant for a good effect.

2 Water all plants an hour before planting.

3 Plant with a trowel or spade if the plant is large, working your way across the border.

4 Return the soil and firm well to remove air pockets.

5 Always water thoroughly unless the weather is wet.

6 Keep root-wrapped plants moist in a cool, shady place until ready to plant out.

7 Remove wrapping and spread the roots out widely in the hole. Water well.

ONE-SIDED HERBACEOUS BORDER

Herbaceous borders are designed to be viewed from one side, the tallest plants at the back and smaller ones at the front. This is a good choice for a narrow garden where an island bed is not possible. A width of 1.2m (4ft) is ideal for access to attend all plants. If possible, leave a narrow access path at the back.

HERBACEOUS PLANTS IN GRAVEL

If you have a gravel garden, try planting bold perennials like verbascum, acanthus, euphorbia or fennel.

GROUND-COVER

Many border perennials make good ground-cover plants, suppress weeds and look attractive.

Some die down in winter but are very pretty for the summer. For evergreen ground-cover try bergenias or epimediums.

ISLAND BEDS

These can be more interesting when there is space. Place the tallest plants in the middle and the smaller radiating towards the edges.

PLANTING AN INVASIVE PLANT

Some grasses and herbaceous plants can be very invasive. Plant them in a large bucket or pot to restrict their spread.

Make drainage holes in the base then sink into the ground so that the rim is level with the surrounding soil.

Put potting compost in the base of the container so that the root ball is at the right level. Firm well, add more compost around the sides and top up the container so that it is hidden.

GROWING HERBACEOUS PLANTS 2

Most herbaceous plants will grow for years without attention, but they will eventually need dividing and replanting. Some benefit from staking, especially in exposed gardens.

DIVIDING AND REPLANTING

DIVIDING FOR PROPAGATION

If propagating more plants, pull the pieces apart by hand in small sections with a shoot and root. Pot them up or grow them on in another piece of ground before replanting.

1 Loosen the clump with a spade or fork, and lift it onto the soil surface.

2 Plants with fibrous roots should be divided with two forks placed back to back.

3 To maintain the plant's vigour, discard the centre of the old plant. Replant only the young pieces from around the edge.

4 Plants with thick fleshy roots may need a spade to chop it into smaller pieces. Divide the crowns with a sharp knife carefully then replant groups of two or three pieces.

5 Small plants can be lifted with a hand fork and pulled apart by hand, or separated with two hand forks.

STAKING PERENNIALS

1 Natural supports such as twiggy sticks are hidden when the plant grows through them. Insert sticks when the plants are just a few centimetres (inches) high, and new shoots will grow through them. If the plant is low growing, bend the tops of the sticks over as shown.

2 Other supports are expensive but last for many years. Styles and sizes vary but they can be clipped together. Insert them before the plant reaches the height of the support.

COMPACT FOLIAGE

Plants with tall flower spikes are vulnerable to wind damage, such as delphiniums, and should be staked with individual canes. Start tying the stem to the cane once the plant is 20–25cm(8–10in) tall.

CUTTING BACK

1 Some plants produce a second and smaller flowering late in the season if they are dead-headed immediately after flowering. Cut the shoots off close to the base with secateurs or shears.

2 Dead-heading plants will make them look tidier. Some look better if they are cut back to ground level after flowering. New foliage will probably grow.

3 Cut back the dead flowered stems at the end of the season. The borders will look tidier and rotting plant material will not encourage overwintering pests and diseases.

KEEPING BORDERS BRIGHT

Shrubs, herbaceous and mixed borders, will look better if a few minutes are spent each week tidying them up. Feeding and watering are not essential, but the display will be more brilliant if you give the plants a boost.

FEEDING AND MULCHING

1 Feed your border plants annually, and shrubs when ever they need a boost. Roses, which are demanding feeders should be fed annually. Sprinkle the fertilizer around the edge of the plants, not over the leaves. Apply it in spring or early summer.

2 Hoe or rake the fertilizer into the top 2.5cm (1in) of soil, remove any that falls on leaves.

3 Water the ground to dissolve the fertilizer, if rain is not forecast.

4 For plants that seem sickly and are not thriving, a foliar feed can be tried. Apply when the sun has moved off the plant by drenching with a fine spray.

5 Mulching helps to suppress weeds and conserve moisture. It also improves the look of the soil. Apply in a layer 5cm (2in) thick to be effective.

SPECIAL NEEDS

Chalky soil will make some plants look yellow. Lime haters such as camellias need to be watered with a chelated iron (Sequestrene) at least once a year. Mix it with water, then apply following the instructions.

As the season progresses, borders can look untidy. Keep the plants watered and fed, and the ground weeded for a smart border like this.

WEEDING

1 Keep the hoe moving around the plants on a dry day, taking the tops off and leaving them to wilt and die.

2 Deep-rooted perennial weeds will regrow if you chop them off at soil level. Dig down and remove the roots completely.

DEAD-HEADING SHRUBS

Many herbaceous plants look better if dead-headed, but large-flowered shrubs such as lilacs also benefit. Take care to remove only the dead flower and not any buds.

END-OF-SEASON CLEAR-UP

1 Cut down the tops of herbaceous plants at the end of the season, unless they are hardy. Gather all the dead stems with a spring-tined lawn rake, and put on the compost heap. Leaving them on the ground will attract disease and slugs.

2 Pick fallen leaves off low ground-cover and rock plants as they block out light and encourage diseases.

PLANT SUPPORTS

Good supports will be hidden once plants have grown, and can make all the difference to whole ranges of plants—from herbaceous perennials to climbers and vegetables such as tomatoes and runner beans.

1 This method is good for runner beans and sweet peas. Insert the canes in angled pairs, then slide a cane through the V formed at the top and tie firmly.

2 A wigwam of canes can be used for runner beans, sweet peas and climbers. Use three to five canes pushed into the ground at an angle and tie firmly.

3 Wigwam cane holders are easy to use. Canes push through the holes in the plastic ring which holds them firmly in place.

PLASTIC CANE GRIPS

Plastic grips can be used to hold the ridge of canes together. One design has two holes for the pairs of canes to be inserted, a horizontal cane is threaded through a plastic loop, which when pulled holds them firmly in place.

Above Metal plants supports are good for border plants with fragile stems. Place the supports early so the plants can grow through them.

SUPPORTING HERBACEOUS PLANTS

1 Twiggy sticks can be used as plant supports if inserted early so the plants can grow up through them.

2 Bend over the twiggy sticks if the plants are small so that they meet in the centre.

3 Insert three or four canes around the clump and secure with twine or string.

4 Chrysanthemums can be supported by the type shown above or net stretched between four canes. Raise the support as the season progresses.

5 Plastic-coated metal supports are more expensive but last for many years. They come in various sizes and and can be linked together.

6 Sometimes it is only the tall flower spikes which need support. Use single canes and tie the stem to the cane as it grows.

F L O W E R S & F O L I A G E

GETTING THROUGH WINTER

Many plants can be saved from the winter cold if they are protected adequately. Frost-tender plants will succumb to frosts no matter where you live, plants that tolerate some frost in one area may be killed off in another area. Take into account the type of winters you experience and protect plants if in doubt.

LIFTING DAHLIAS

1 Lift dahlia tubers, with a fork, once the frost has blackened the foliage.

2 Stand the tubers upside down in a dry frost-free place. This will help moisture to drain from the hollow stems, and reduce the risk of rotting later.

3 Once the tubers are dry, pack them in boxes of peat, or other insulating material, and keep in a frost-proof place for the winter. Label the tubers individually if storing more than one variety.

PROTECTING VULNERABLE SHRUBS

1 Protect valuable shrubs of borderline hardiness with a winter wrap. Make a frame of canes, cover with polythene or layers of horticultural fleece to make a form of tent.

2 Protect tender wall shrubs with a shield of conifer branches.

ALPINES

Alpines grow in cold winter areas, but are prone to waterlogging. You can protect vulnerable alpines with a sheet of glass held in a wire frame, or on bricks, above the plants.

STORING TENDER BULBS

1 Lift gladioli and vulnerable bulbs before there are penetrating frosts. Use a fork to remove them and dry them off before storing. Bulblets or cormlets formed around the bases, should be stored separately.

2 Dust the bulbs with a fungicide—or dip them into a fungicidal solution, then leave to dry again.

3 Pack in paper (not plastic) bags, or nets, and keep in a frost-free place. Don't forget to label them.

SUMMER BEDDING

When you buy your summer bedding plants or raise them yourself, plant them with imagination as well as care. Do not plant them out until all danger of frost has passed and make sure they have been hardened off. Be guided by your local parks department, if in doubt when to plant.

PLANTING IN DRIFTS

1 Plant in drifts for a bold effect. Bold splashes of colour look better than mixed plants together. Mark out a basic pattern before you plant.

2 Water the trays half an hour before planting, to ensure the compost is thoroughly moist.

3 Remove plants carefully and lay them on the soil to set the spacing. Adjust the space according to each plant's needs.

4 Dig a hole with a trowel and plant deeper than the depth of the seed tray. Firm in place to reduce the risk of the roots drying out.

5 Water well and continue to water in dry weather until the plants become established.

TIPS FOR BRIGHT BEDDING SCHEMES

Dot plants, sometimes called spot plants, are used to give height to a bed of low-growing plants. These can be other flowering plants or silver leaved foliage plants. Fuchias are sometimes used, but try any plant that is bold and contrasts well with others.

Carpet bedding (below) uses flowering and foliage plants to create geometric, abstract, or theme designs in a formal way. You can try this in a small garden with dwarf bedding plants like lobelia, alyssum and French marigolds.

Island beds look good planted with a formal design, with a tall feature in the centre.
Informal grouping (below) appeals to gardeners who dislike formality. Interplant two, three or four plants so that they grow into each other.

Bedding plants don't have to be bold or even used in a formal bed. Here they are in a predominately white scheme in front of shrubs.

SPRING BEDDING

Clear summer bedding, as soon as it has finished, and replant for a spring display.

PLANTING SPRING BEDDING PLANTS

1 Lift the remains of the summer bedding, then fork over the ground. If necessary, apply bonemeal.

2 Remove all weeds, rake in the fertilizer if used, and level the ground ready for planting.

3 **Above** Water plants well half an hour before lifting.

4 **Above right** Lift with as much soil as possible, firming it into a ball around the roots.

5 **Right** Plant with a trowel checking that the spacing looks right as you go.

MIXED BEDDING SCHEMES

If planting more than one kind of bedding plant, allow plenty of space when you plant the first type. Then lay out the second choice to check spacing.

Fully plant a small area at a time, otherwise it will be difficult to avoid treading on young plants.

BULBS

Bulbs interplanted with spring bedding plants look good and extend the period of interest.

Plant the bulbs between the young plants as you go along, to avoid having to step on them.

A LAWN FROM SEED

Sowing a lawn is cheaper than making one from turf and will establish quickly if sown at the right time— in spring or early autumn. Regular watering will be needed if sowing takes place in the summer.

PREPARING THE GROUND

1 Level the ground, by raking down from the top of the levelling pegs. Check the level of the pegs with a spirit level.

2 Firm the soil by treading it to remove air pockets. Shuffle your feet over the area, first one way, then the next.

THE RIGHT TYPE OF SEED

Different seed mixtures are suitable for different tasks. Hard-wearing seed will contain ryegrass, decorative lawn seed will not. Lawns with ryegrass can look good and wear well.

These trial plots show how cultivation is as important as the seed. The left plots are a ryegrass mix, the plots on the right are without ryegrass. The top plots have been treated with weedkiller, but the bottom ones have not.

3 Rake the soil to a fine, crumbly structure. Leave for a couple of weeks to allow any weed seedlings to germinate, then hoe or use a weed-killer, safe for replanting in a few days. Rake once more.

SOWING GRASS SEED

1 Mark out the area into 1m (1yd) strips with pegs and string. Divide each strip into 1m (1yd) sections, using canes as guides.

2 Use a small container to measure out the amount of seed for 1 square metre (1 square yard). Apply to one square at a time, in alternate directions.

3 It is worth hiring a seed distributor if the area to sow is large. Once it has been calibrated to release the correct amount of seed, simply push the distributor over the ground.

4 Rake the surface lightly, and in dry weather, use a lawn sprinkler to keep seeds moist.

Nothing sets off beds of flowers as well as a smart well groomed lawn.

A LAWN FROM TURF

For an 'instant result' use turf to give you a usable lawn in a couple of months. You can lay turf at most times of the year if you avoid frozen ground and water in dry weather. Spring and early autumn are good times. Prepare the ground as for sowing seed.

LAYING TURF

1 Lay the first row against a straight edge. Butt each turf close against the previous piece.

2 Stagger each row like brickwork. Kneel on a plank to avoid damaging the turves.

3 Roll the plank forward as you lay further rows.

4 Tamp the turf down with the back of a rake or garden roller, to remove any air.

5 Brush sieved sandy soil or a mixture of peat and sand into the joints, to bind them together.

CREATING A CURVED EDGE

Peg down a hosepipe or rope with bent wire to create a curved edge. Use this as a guide to trim with an edging iron. Keep the grass moist in dry weather and until it is well established.

6 Use an edging iron to trim the edges if needed. Stand on a plank of wood to keep the edge straight.

MAKING OUT AN OVAL BED

1 Getting the proportions right is trial and error, start by marking out a rectangle.

2 Use string to check that the diagonals are the same length. Place pegs centrally along each side and stretch string between them.

Above Make beds and borders look smart by ensuring a neat edge. Take special care when cutting out curved beds.

3 Cut a piece of string half the length of the oval, between the top and bottom pegs. Use a side peg as a pivot to indicate where to insert other pegs.

4 Cut a piece of string twice the distance between one of these pegs and the top or bottom of the oval, whichever is furthest away. Make a loop from the string.

5 Drape a loop over the two inner pegs then mark a line on the grass in sand, keeping the string taut. Cut an outline of the oval with an edging iron, lift the turf with a spade.

ROUTINE LAWN CARE

Lawns are often the largest and dominant feature of the garden throughout the year. A neglected lawn can mar your garden, but one that is well-cared for will set off all the other features.

SPRING LAWN CARE

1 Use a mechanical spreader, as above, to feed your lawn easily. Spreading by hand requires the area to be divided into squares.

2 If the lawn is full of weeds, apply lawn weedkiller in mid or late spring. Use a dribble bar and mark off the areas treated to avoid over-dosing.

3 For a few weeds, spot treatment may be used. Brush or dab on a selective lawn weed-killer.

4 Rake or brush off debris. These will not harm the lawn but may provide a seed bed for weeds to grow in.

5 Trimming the edges makes the lawn look better. Long-handled shears are slow but make a neat job. An electric edge trimmer or line trimmer will do the job quickly.

6 Bare areas should be reseeded. Loosen the surface, sprinkle on patch seed. Water well and cover with plastic until the seeds germinate.

AUTUMN LAWN CARE

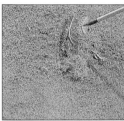

1 Rake the lawn to remove the 'thatch' of dead grass and old clippings, and moss.

2 A powered lawn rake will make the job much easier on a large lawn. A powered slitter, like this, will aerated a large lawn.

3 After raking, aerate the lawn. A tool that removes cores of soil is ideal but on small lawns, a fork will do.

4 Brush sand into the holes if your lawn soil is heavy clay. If your soil is sandy, brush in peat instead.

5 If the lawn is in poor condition, apply an autumn lawn feed. Do not use spring or summer feed as the fresh growth will be killed off by frost.

6 Use a moss killer for autumn use, if it is a problem. Lawn sand is unsuitable for this time of year, as it contains fertilizer.

7 Straighten uneven edges with an edging iron against a straight edge of timber. Do not do this too often as the lawn reduces in size each time.

DEALING WITH LAWN PROBLEMS

Bumps and hollows make mowing difficult, and broken edges leave the lawn unsightly. These can be repaired leaving it good as new.

REDUCING WEAR

Protect an area from concentrated wear, by pegging down a piece of mesh or netting. The grass will grow through it but the netting will protect wear on the actual surface.

BUMPS AND HOLLOWS

1 Use an edging iron or a spade to cut a cross through the centre of the area. Extend the cuts beyond the bump or hollow.

2 Use a spade to slice through the soil beneath the grass, so that you can lift it up to roll it back.

3 Roll back the four cut pieces to expose the soil beneath.

4 Remove soil if there is a bump, or top up if there is a hollow.

5 Level the soil as evenly as you can, then roll back the turf. If the level is not good, then lift the affected part and adjust.

6 Firm the grass with the back of a spade, or tread it in by standing on a plank. Trickle fine soil into the joints, then water well.

REPAIRING A BROKEN EDGE

1 Use an edging iron or a spade to cut a rectangle around the affected area.

2 Push a spade under the grass, starting at the edge and keeping the slice of grass as even as possible.

3 Reverse the turf so the broken edge is on the inside.

4 Fill the hole with sifted soil, then sow grass seed.

5 Brush sifted soil into the joints to help them knit.

6 After watering, cover the reseeded patch until the seed has germinated.

ROCK GARDENS 1

On a sunny site, even a small rock garden will enable you to grow a large collection of plants in a small space. With an island bed you can make a rock garden in your lawn, or build one in a corner of your garden.

MAKING A ROCK GARDEN

1 Choose a sunny site—sloping if possible but it can be made on flat ground by building a mound. Remove all weeds.

2 Lay a layer of hardcore as a foundation to aid drainage. Tip garden soil over this to a depth of 15–30cm (6–12in).

3 Cover the low mound of soil with inverted turves, to provide a base for the special soil mix.

4 Alpine plants prefer a mix of equal parts soil, coarse grit and peat. This suits most plants.

5 Mix the three ingredients well, turning them until they are blended together.

6 Mark out the area you want the final rock garden to occupy with string and pile the soil mixture to the height of the second layer of rocks.

7 Remove the string, then lay the rocks at ground level. Add more soil to to the back and sides to stabilize the rocks.

8 Add the second layer of rocks, keeping the grain of the rock (strata) in the same direction. Use a pole or crowbar to lever them into place.

9 Manipulate rocks with rollers or levers as they can be very heavy.

10 Add soil as each layer is built up, this will increase the height for the next row.

11 Make the sides slope and build towards a flattish summit with a nice rock laid on top.

12 Finish off with a layer of coarse sand or horticultural grit.

13 The rock garden will look much better if it is sited in a corner, with a backdrop of plants such as dwarf conifers.

ROCK GARDENS 2: PLANTING AND CARE

FLOWERS & FOLIAGE

A rock garden can soon look neglected unless you plant carefully, avoiding vigorous plants. Trim back plants and make sure weeds are kept under control.

2 Water the plants and let them drain before planting. Knock them out of their pots, holding your hand over the root ball.

3 Use a narrow blade trowel to dig a larger hole then the root ball.

PLANTING A ROCK GARDEN

1 Space out the plants in their pots before you begin to plant. This lets you visualize the overall effect and makes it easier to alter plant positions.

4 Pour gritty soil around the roots, making sure the crown is not too deep.

5 After firming, trickle more grit around the plant, avoiding touching the leaves.

6 Firm and level the grit to create a pleasing finish.

KEEPING THE PLANTS LOOKING GOOD

1 Always remove weeds when they are small, or they will smother small alpines.

2 **Right** Perennial weeds growing between rocks will be difficult to remove. Try applying a translocated weedkiller which will kill the roots and the leaves. Be very careful not to touch plants you wish to keep.

3 Slugs and snails will be deterred by coarse grit or chippings. Sprinkle pellets around vulnerable plants.

STONE CHIPPING DRESSINGS

A dressing of stone chippings will need to be topped up or renewed eventually. They get washed away and the soil works its way through. Make sure you place some beneath the collar of each plant so the leaves are kept off the wet soil.

CUTTING BACK

In the spring, cut off any dead shoots killed during the winter. Many alpines will remain more compact and vigorous if the dead flowering shoots are cut off with shears.

PLANTING IN WALLS AND PAVING CREVICES

Make the most of all available planting spaces by packing a dry wall with interesting alpines and planting between the paving too,

PLANTING IN PAVING

1 Chisel out a few crevices if your crazy paving is mortared to a depth of at least 5cm (2in).

2 Ready made crevices should be cleared of old soil and filled with loam-based compost.

3 Use small plants or seedlings and tease most of the compost away to make insertion easier.

4 Trickle more compost around the roots after planting.

5 Firm gently with your fingers to remove air pockets.

6 Water carefully with a fine mist from a compression sprayer. This will not wash the compost away. Water regularly until they are established.

7 Sowing alpine seeds directly into the crevices is worth trying. Sprinkle a few seeds onto compost, cover with more compost and water as before.

PLANTING A DRY STONE WALL

1 Plant small seedlings or cuttings in the crevices, even small spaces can be planted this way.

2 Press moist compost into the space to cover the roots with a pencil or dibber to avoid air pockets.

3 If the compost falls out press a few small stones into the space to hold it in.

4 Keep the plants and compost moist by spraying with a fine mist. Once established, they will not need regular watering.

5 Try sowing a few alpines directly into the wall, by mixing with compost in your hand.

6 Moisten the seed/compost mix and press into a suitable crevice. Choose robust alpines such as aubrieta.

Many alpines can be grown in crevices in the side of a dry stone wall, but even if the wall is mortared you can create a similar effect by planting vigorous trailers like aubrieta to spill over the edge.

A GARDEN FOR WILDLIFE

If you love wildlife, modify your garden to encourage birds and butterflies. Wild flowers can be looked upon as food sources for wildlife instead of as weeds —many are as pretty as cultivated plants.

SOWING AND PLANTING WILD FLOWERS

1 The easiest method to produce a wild flower meadow, is to sow a special mixture on prepared ground. The wild flowers will find it easier to become established if you start from scratch.

2 Specialist nurseries sell wild flower plants. Buy these to save time and trouble.

LONG GRASS AND WILD FLOWERS

Leave part of the lawn unmown and unweeded, to add 'texture' in a large lawn. This will look acceptable in a small lawn if you leave the grass long around a tree in a corner. Cut with shears in the autumn when the flowers have finished blooming.

3 Plant the seedlings as soon as possible after unpacking, and plant according to needs.

NURSERY-BED WILD FLOWERS

To plant wild flowers in an established lawn or a wild area, sow the seeds like cultivated plants and grow in a nursery bed until large enough to plant out.

You can buy wild flower seed mixtures that are every bit as bright as highly bred plants— and attract wildlife too.

MAKING A MINI-POND

Make a mini-pool to encourage pondlife, if you don't have a proper pond.

You can make one out of a half barrel or plastic tub, sinking it into the soil or leaving it above ground.

Make sure that the container is level and leave the top just above soil level to reduce the risk of soil falling in.The

barrel can be lined with a pond liner if it leaks, or repair it with sealing mastic.

You can make a mini-pool for birds and animals to drink from with an old dustbin lid. Sink it flush with the ground, and mask the edge with stones or plants. Keep it topped up with water throughout the summer.

WINDOWBOXES

Make a really bold box with a single-colour or single-subject planting, or make it subdued and have foliage predominating. Don't leave your windowboxes empty at the end of the autumn—this is the time to plant them up with spring bulbs.

PLANTING A SUMMER WINDOWBOX

1 Place a layer of broken clay pots over the drainage holes. If you don't have any of these, use coarsely chipped bark.

2 Partly fill the box with good compost. Use loam-based compost, as it is less prone to drying out and starvation. Adding water-absorbing crystals (see Planting a Hanging Basket) will help conserve moisture.

3 Buy pot-grown plants although costing more, they make better plants more quickly. Space the plants whilst still in their pots. Adjust if necessary. Space foliage plants along the box— one will look like a mistake.

4 Make sure that the plants have been watered first, then knock them out of their pots and plant. Trickle compost between them to fill any gaps. Firm gently. Water thoroughly and place in position.

144

PLANTING A SPRING WINDOWBOX

1 Bulbs need less feeding than summer plants. You can re-use some of the old summer compost and mix it with fresh compost. Wash out the box with garden disinfectant first.

2 Place pieces of broken clay pots or coarsely chipped bark over the holes to allow for drainage.

3 Add just enough compost to cover the bottom few centimetres (inches).

4 Place larger bulbs, such as daffodils, at this deeper level.

5 Add more compost so that the larger bulbs are almost covered. Then plant smaller bulbs such as scillas or crocuses between them. Cover with more compost.

6 For winter flowering, pansies or forget-me-nots, can be planted before finally topping up with compost. The bulbs will grow through them.

HANGING BASKETS

While you are planting out your windowboxes, be sure to plant a few hanging baskets too— they're challenging but make a real welcome at the front door.

PLANTING A HANGING BASKET

1 Line a basket with damp sphagnum moss, to where the first plants will be placed.

2 You can add water-absorbing crystals to the compost to aid moisture retention in hot weather.

3 Add compost to the level of the moss. Insert seedlings through the mesh, trying to keep compost around the roots.

4 Add more compost, plant another layer, then fill to just below the rim. Put a bold plant in the centre of a mixed basket.

5 Fill in any gaps. Water well. Do not hang up immediately. Keep in a sheltered place for a week to let plants settle.

146

PLANTING A HALF-BASKET

1 Line with moss and plant as described for a normal basket. Propping the basket on small pots will be helpful.

2 Plant the top last, then hang on a wall in a porch or sheltered spot until established. Move to its final position after a week or two.

BASKET LINERS

Moss makes an attractive liner, but many proprietary liners are available. Although less attractive, once the plants bush out, you will hardly notice them. Choose one which allows side planting unless you only want to plant the top.

Once the plants are fully established, take the basket outside. They are usually hung from chains on a bracket which can be fixed to a fence post.

F
L
O
W
E
R
S
&
F
O
L
I
A
G
E

147

TUBS AND TROUGHS

Tubs and troughs will add colour to dull parts of the patio, and bring life to a balcony. Try planting a permanent container with a selection of year-round interest plants such as alpines.

PLANTING A TUB OR URN

1 Place pieces of broken clay post, or coarsely chipped bark o cover the holes.

2 If weight is a problem, use a peat-based compost, otherwise use a loam-based compost.

3 Place a tall, bold plant in the centre, as a focal point, in both perennial and summer displays.

4 Plant some trailers around the edge to take the eye downwards. Small-leaved ivies are good but you could use a flowering trailer for a summer display.

5 Top up the container with compost after planting and water well. A dressing of chipped bark or cocoa shells will improve the appearance.

MOVING TUBS

Reconstituted stone and concrete tubs and urns are very heavy. Always get help to move them.

Right A decorative tub can enhance the display of flowers. Don't spoil the effect with too many trailers. This one is planted with geraniums, a fuchsia, and *Helichrysum petiolatum*.

PLANTING AN ALPINE TROUGH

1 Choose pot grown plants and an attractive trough. Lay broken clay pots at the bottom and top up with gritty loam-based compost. Space out the plants.

2 Remove plants and some of the compost around the root ball if necessary. Plant the alpines at the same depth as they were originally planted.

3 To improve the appearance of the planted trough, sprinkle some stone chippings or fine gravel over the compost.

Right A sink garden looks better if small rocks are placed among the alpines.

PLANTING A BARREL

1 If you have a large area to dig such as a vegetable plot, or a new garden to cultivate, divide it into two equal areas. Then you can dig to one end.

2 Plant three clematis (or other climbers) at a slight inward angle.

3 Insert three canes so they cross at the top. Tie together with twine or use a cane holder.

4 Tie the plants to the canes. Once they reach the top, they will become self-supporting

TREES AND SHRUBS IN TUBS

Give your patio a touch of distinction by growing a few trees and shrubs in large pots. They are easy to look after and many look attractive all year round.

PLANTING A TREE

1 Right Choose a large container—at least 30cm (12in) in diameter. Make sure it is frostproof. Insert a drainage layer before adding loam-based compost, which has the weight to support a tree in windy weather. Fill so that the top of the root ball is 2.5–5cm (1–2) below the rim.

2 Left Remove the tree from its container and stand it on the new compost. Trickle more around the sides.

3 A tree will offer a lot of wind resistance, so ram the compost firmly around the root ball to ensure stability.

PLANTING SHRUBS

1 Single specimen shrubs can be planted but a collection of dwarf shrubs with contrasting or colourful foliage will be attractive for a longer period. Stand the plants in a group first to see how they look together.

Right Groups of shrubs can be as effective as one shrub.

TREES IN TUBS

If the base of the tree looks bare plant it with shade loving plants such as ivies, spring bulbs or sow some quick and easy hardy annuals until the tree is established.

A SUITABLE COMPOST

Use a loam-based compost for trees and shrubs. If you are growing lime hating shrubs they will need an ericaceous mix. This will be more acidic then other types of compost.

2 Plant firmly, ensuring they are at their original depth in the compost.

3 Cover visible compost with a mulch of gravel, cocoa shells or expanded clay granules.

CARING FOR PLANTS IN CONTAINERS

If you look after your containers, they will reward you with healthy growth and a good show. Neglecting feeding and watering will bring disappointing results. The benefits of care and attention can be seen and enjoyed.

FEEDING YOUR PLANTS

1 If you can't remember to feed regularly, try placing a sachet of slow-release fertilizer beneath each plant.

2 Slow-release fertilizer can be added to the compost, releasing its nutrients when the weather is warm.

WATERING YOUR PLANTS

1 An automatic watering system is ideal for containers close together on a patio. Run a small drip tube from the main supply pipe, adjust the flow rate.

2 A hosepipe is the easiest way to water a lot of containers. Fit an outside tap and run piping to parts of the garden so a hose can be attached.

3 Use a lance attachment fitted to a hose, compression sprayer, or basket pump to water hanging baskets.

4 An alternative to a lance, is to tie the end of a hose to a garden cane. This holds the hose rigid so you can hold it up to a basket.

3 Soluble and liquid fertilizers are quick-acting and produce rapid results. Feed regularly at the rate recommended.

4 Remember to feed trees and shrubs, as the compost must sustain a lot of growth over a long period. Sprinkle slow-release fertilizer over the surface in spring and then fork it in.

ROUTINE CARE

1 Many summer bedding plants cease flowering early if you allow the flowers to set seed. Dead-head plants with large flowers, they will look tidier and will flower for longer.

2 Give summer bedding plants a health check once a week. Remove yellowing leaves and those affected by disease or pests, unless you can control them by sprays.

3 Control pests and diseases promptly as close planting can cause the problems to spread quickly. Systemic insecticides and fungicides are the most effective.

x

F L O W E R S & F O L I A G E

MAKING A POND

Old-fashioned concrete ponds used to be difficult to construct, but with modern liners and pre-formed pools, making a pond is a job you can complete in a weekend.

1 Insert canes around the edge and lay rope around them to transfer the shape to the ground.

2 Dig out the shape as carefully as possible. Check on the shape by laying the pond in the hole regularly. Making the hole a few centimetres (9inches) larger than the actual pond, will make backfilling easier later.

3 Lay wood across the hole to check the level and measure down from this.

4 Put the pool in the hole and check that it is level.

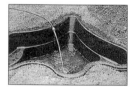

5 Run water into the pool, as the level rises, pack fine soil around the edge.

6 Pack soil with wood, firmly beneath the shelves to avoid causing stresses within the moulding. Check the level as you fill and pack.

MARGINAL SHELVES

Waterlilies prefer the deeper water in the centre, most aquatic plants grow in shallow water. A marginal shelf will let you grow many kinds of plants.

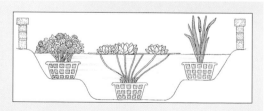

FLOWERS & FOLIAGE

A LINER POND

1 Use a length of hosepipe to mark out the shape or your pond. If doing the job in winter, run hot water through the hose to make it more supple.

2 Dig out soil to the right depth. Leave a shallow ledge 23cm (9in) wide halfway down the total depth of the pool. Remove grass from the edge deep enough for the thickness of the paving and the mortar.

3 Make sure that the edge of the pond is level. Space pegs 90–120cm (3–4ft) apart around the edge. Go around the pool with a spirit-level.

4 Put a layer of sand 12mm (0.5in) on the bottom and the marginal shelves, and the sides if possible. If the soil is very stony, use a polyester mat instead of sand.

5 Drape the liner loosely in the hole, making sure that there is enough overlap all around. Hold the edges in place with a few bricks. Run in water from a hosepipe.

6 Lift the bricks from around the edge and let the liner move a little as the liner fills up with water. There will be creases, remove these by stretching and adjusting the liner.

7 Once filled, cut off surplus liner, leaving a flap of about 15cm (6in) all way round. This will be covered and held in place by the mortar and paving.

8 Bed a paved edge on a mortar bed of three parts sand to one part cement. Crazy-paving or rectangular slabs can be used around the edge of an irregular shape like this.

STOCKING THE POND

The best time to stock the pond with plants is mid spring to early summer. Do not put any tender floating aquatics in until there is no risk of frost. Add fish at any time, but wait for a few weeks if the pond is recently planted.

PLANTING A WATERLILY

1 Although you can plant waterlilies in special planting baskets, an old washing-up bowl holds more compost and has room for expansion.

2 Always add oxygenating plants. These can be planted around the edges or in their own containers.

3 Cover the compost surface with gravel to help anchor the plants down, It will also reduce the chance of fish stirring up mud in the water.

4 If early in the season, the waterlilies will have short stems, so sit the container on bricks. Once the stems have grown, remove the bricks and sit the container at the bottom of the pond.

PLANTING MARGINAL AQUATICS

1 Buy a special planting basket, and line it with turf, or a special liner, to hold in the compost.

2 Put the plant in the container, adding compost in the bottom if the plant is small. Add more compost free of fertilizer.

3 Cover with gravel to anchor the plant and keep the compost in place.

4 Gently lower the basket into the water so that it sits on one of the marginal shelves. Make sure that the top of the basket is covered with water.

ADDING FISH

2 Release the fish by opening the bag and letting them swim free. Do not keep the fish for too long in the bag as they may be starved of oxygen.

1 Float the bag on the surface for a couple of hours so that the temperatures equalize. Never release fish straight into the pond when you get them home.

FLOATING PLANTS
Some aquatics float, and only need placing on the surface.

POND MAINTENANCE

FLOWERS & FOLIAGE

You will need to spend a couple of hours in the spring and autumn to keep the water sparkling and the plants healthy. If you stock fish, be prepared to keep a small area free of ice in freezing weather.

CLEANING THE POND

1 Thoroughly clean the pond after two or three years. The pond pump will empty most of the water. Use a bucket to finish emptying the water.

2 Once the water level is low, the fish will be easier to catch. Keep them in containers filled with the old pond water. Cover with netting to stop them jumping out.

3 Remove all plants, scrub off the dirt and mud, then rinse with a hose. Scoop out the dirty water with a bucket.

4 Refill with tap water, which contains chlorine harmful to fish, so keep the fish away for a few days before returning them.

5 Take the opportunity to divide and repot overcrowded plants.

6 Pull or cut each plant apart to make several smaller pieces.

7 Repot each portion. Remember to cover the surface of the compost or pot with gravel before replacing in the pond.

SPRING AND SUMMER POND CARE

1 Algae will usually disappear once the larger plants are growing well, absorbing nutrients and shading the water, but chemical controls are available and you should follow the instructions very carefully.

2 Reduce blanket weed, by twisting it around a cane or stick. This algae can also be controlled with an algicide.

AUTUMN POND CARE

1 Rake out leaves before they sink and start to rot. You can use a lawn rake but be careful if you have a pond liner.

3 Trim off dying leaves from marginal plants or those on the edge of the pond, to reduce the amount of vegetation that may rot during the winter.

2 Rake out some of the plants which have become overgrown.

4 Cover the pond with netting to stop more leaves falling in. Once leaf fall has passed, remove the netting.

WINTER POND CARE

1 Float tennis balls on the pond surface if frost is forecast. The balls will provide small ice-free areas. This method is only for short cold spells.

2 To release toxic gases built up in a frozen pond, stand a pan of hot water on the ice. Tie a string to the handle so that you can retrieve it, if it sinks.

3 Use a pond heater to keep it ice-free. It costs no more than a large light bulb to run. There are mains and low-voltage versions.

GREENHOUSE BASICS

A basic greenhouse is simply a protective shell which you need to equip to display the plants well and provide extra growing space. Adding an automatic ventilator opener should be regarded as an essential, not an optional extra.

INSTALLING AN AUTOMATIC VENTILATOR

1 Automatic ventilators are quick and easy to install. Follow the instructions carefully as products vary. This one is first fixed to the centre of the manual ventilator.

2 The other end of the bracket is bolted to the frame.

3 Finally, the opener will need adjusting so that it opens and closes at the right temperature.

HIGH VENTILATORS

If you buy a greenhouse with a high manual ventilator, difficult to reach, make sure that an easy-winder is also supplied.

FIXING A SHELF

1 Shelves are invaluable as they provide extra growing space. Aluminium greenhouse shelves come in kits that you assemble yourself. They should be supplied with brackets that bolt together and fix to the frame.

2 Assemble all brackets for the shelves first, and use a spirit-level to check they are all level.

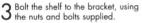

3 Bolt the shelf to the bracket, using the nuts and bolts supplied.

4 End pieces are available to make a better finish and reduce the dangers from sharp metal corners.

ASSEMBLING AN INTEGRATED BENCH

1 Fitted benches come with most metal greenhouses as an optional extra. They are worth buying as they will suit the size of the greenhouse. Follow the instructions, but they will probably bolt to the existing frame.

2 Check the levels of each length of surface. Adjust at this stage, before you finish assembling the surface.

GETTING THE BEST FROM YOUR GREENHOUSE

The greenhouse can be used to propagate many garden plants, tomatoes, cucumbers and other vegetables.

In winter you need to insulate to keep it warm; in summer you'll need to ventilate and shade it to keep it cool.

THERMAL SCREENS

A thermal screen will conserve heat if you pull it across at night. Hang it on wires that run along the eaves. Just push it to one end in the morning, and pull it across at night.

If you want to reduce costs by heating just part of the greenhouse, separate it vertically with plastic sheeting. You may be able to buy a special kit.

INSULATING A GREENHOUSE

1 In a metal greenhouse, buy clips that you insert first, then hold the polythene in place either by snapping or pushing in a cap. Adhesive tape can seal the overlaps.

2 In a timber-framed greenhouse, pin the insulation to the glazing bars with drawing pins.

3 Always insulate the ventilators separately so that they can be opened. Ventilation is important in an insulated greenhouse to avoid diseases caused by high humidity.

162

SHADING A GREENHOUSE

1 Paint-on shading is a cheap and easy way to reduce the scorching effects of the summer sun.

2 To save time if the greenhouse is large, spray it on. Avoid the spray drifting over the glazing bars.

3 At the end of the summer, remove the shading with a duster or cloth when its dry.

4 Internal shading is not as effective but is better than none. Fix plastic net to the inside of the glazing bars, with clips used for insulation.

EXTERIOR ROLLER BLINDS

These are very effective, and more flexible than a paint-on wash as you can remove or apply shading to suit the weather.

HOW TO MAKE A CAPILLARY BENCH

1 To make a capillary bench fix a length of plastic gutter to the edge and lay a sheet of polythene over the bench.

2 Cut a length of capillary matting, available from garden centres, to size leaving one edge to fold into the gutter. Top up the gutter with water by hand.

WATERING THE GREENHOUSE

FLOWERS & FOLIAGE

Watering is the most demanding aspect of greenhouse gardening—it is a daily chore for much of the year. You can make life much easier if you install an automatic watering system.

INSTALLING A CAPILLARY BENCH

Lay capillary matting over the whole bench. Cut matting to size, do not leave any trailing over the edge, as it may drain water away.

You can make your own reservoir using a ball valve, but it is easier to buy one designed for the job which can be connected to the mains. If this is not possible, buy one designed for use with a bag (the hose connector will be a different size).

Use the matting as a wick to draw water from the reservoir to the bench matting.

HAND-WATERING

1 Press your finger into the surface to judge if the moisture level is adequate.

2 Alternatively, use a moisture indicator in a few pots as a guide.

OVERHEAD SPRAYING

If you prefer a spray system, buy one that can be suspended from the roof. Nozzles are screwed into the tubing at intervals. Some can spray on both sides or just one side of the greenhouse.

IMPROVISING

You can improvise reservoirs. This system uses a length of plastic gutter as a reservoir, into which one end of the matting is inserted. Keep the gutter topped up with water by hand, from a cistern, or dip fed by a water bag.

Bottom picture Capillary
benches are not suitable for
seedling and cuttings which
need to be watered by hand.

3 Plants in large pots are best
watered without a rose on
the can, using a finger on the
end to reduce the flow.

4 Water seedlings with a rose
on the can, facing upwards
when they are small so that the
water falls more gently.

DISPLAYING AND CARING FOR GREENHOUSE PLANTS

FLOWERS & FOLIAGE

Arranging your pots attractively, will keep your greenhouse looking good. Feed, water them, and maintain the correct humidity.

MAKING THE MOST OF SHELVES

Shelves are good for trays of seedlings in spring and to display pot plants during the summer. Take care not to shade the plants below too much.

HANGING SHELVES

Shelves can be fixed from either the roof glazing bars or by brackets to the side glazing bars. Choose a suitable type.

POT PLANTS

Try growing pot plants in a group by growing them, in their pots, in the greenhouse border rather than on shelving.

STAGING DISPLAYS

1 Build your displays in different heights to make a striking show. Pots can be stood upon empty pots... use trailers at the front to cascade over the edge.

2 Tiered staging makes the most of usable space. Use the bottom shelves for resting plants or as storage.

3 Self-watering containers can be used for display in the greenhouse. Plant a large tub with bold feature plants or one striking plant such as this aubergine.

Although this is larger than most green-houses, the same kind of display can be achieved on a more modest scale.

CLIMBERS

On a lean-to-greenhouse, paint the back wall white to reflect light and use a back ground for wall shrubs and climbers. Plant in the border and train them up wires fixed to the back wall.

CREATING THE RIGHT ATMOSPHERE

1 Fit one automatic ventilator so the temperature never becomes too high. Open more ventilators or open the door to keep the greenhouse cool.

2 Plants prefer humid atmos-pheres so when the tempera-ture is hot, damp down the paths with a watering-can to increase humidity.

COLD FRAMES

Cold frames are invaluable for overwintering vulnerable plants, if you don't have a greenhouse. They can also be used as an overflow in late spring or for hardening off seedlings before you plant them out. To get the best from your frame, insulate it against severe frosts.

ERECTING A COLD FRAME FROM A KIT

1 Aluminium kits are easy to make, they come with all that you will need, including glass. Check that all the parts are there when you open the box.

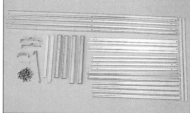

3 When the main frame is completed, insert the glass. It is held in place with clips or glazing strips. Slide or fix on the tops, making sure they lift or slide easily.

2 Bolt the frame together in the order suggested.

INSULATING A COLD FRAME

1 Glass and aluminium frames will be colder than brick-walled ones. For more protection, insulate the sides with expanded polystyrene.

2 Cut the sides, allowing for the thickness at each end. Push into place so that they are a tight fit. If loose, wedge pieces of card in at one end to hold them in position.

TYPES OF COLD FRAME

Aluminium frames are widely available in kit form and easy to make. They are glazed to the ground, letting in more light. They quickly loose heat through the sides unless you insulate them in the winter.

Wooden frames do come as kits but are more expensive and less widely available. You can make your own and make it blend in with the garden better than a metal one can.

Brick-walled frames are seldom used by amateurs as they are more difficult to construct. They do protect plants better than thin-walled frames.

INSULATING AND VENTILATION

1 Never insulate the top of a frame permanently, unless using bubble polythene, as the plants need light. On very cold nights a covering can be used but needs removing the next day.

2 Good ventilation is essential in warm weather, even in the winter. Sliding tops are useful as they are less prone to wind damage.

3 Lifting tops sometimes have an adjustable device. A simple wedge can be made with notches so that you can open the top by different amounts as the plants are hardened off.

FRUIT & VEGETABLES

The kitchen garden holds its own special charm; a bed of ripening vegetables, clusters of tomatoes catching the sun, and crisp rows of salad crops all look as good as they taste. Add a few decorative herbs and some cordon fruits, and this part of the garden will compare well with the ornamental area.

Opposite
The produce of the kitchen can look good as well as taste good. Apples like these 'Sunset' look particularly appetizing.

INTRODUCTION

Fruit, vegetables and herbs are rewarding to grow. The results of your hard work are enjoyed on your dinner plate. Many herbs are highly ornamental and worth growing in the flower garden even if of no culinary use.

The kitchen garden is particularly labour-intensive, and the difference between a mediocre and bumper crop can be accounted for by the amount of care and attention

it has received. Many of the tips in the following pages will help you to achieve better or bigger crops, and extend the harvesting season.

An early start can produce crops weeks ahead of the normal time, yielding home-grown produce at a time when it is more expensive in the shops. Cloches, floating cloches and horticultural fleece are among techniques described and there are hints

Above Marrows and courgettes need space, but a single plant is useful.

Left 'Doyenne du Comice' is grown as a tree but can be trained as a cordon or espalier.

Left Kitchen gardens were dedicated to fruit, vegetables and herbs in the past, but don't despair if space is limited. A worthwhile collection can be grown even in a small plot.

Left Crops of strawberries are within everyone's reach.

Below Enjoy apples like these 'Idared'.

for extending the season into late autumn plus ideas for storing what you can't eat fresh.

There are tips on extra crops you can harvest once the main harvest has been collected.

Growing vegetables can be fun too, and even though you can't feed a family from a few windowboxes or containers on the patio, it is rewarding to harvest early potatoes from a growing bag, or pick pretty red-leaved lettuces from a windowbox.

A crop of onions is easy to grow from seed. Grow plenty to store for winter use.

You will find plenty of ideas for growing herbs and vegetables in containers in the greenhouse and outdoors.

Fruit trees are not only for orchards, they can be trained to grow against a wall or fence, and there are fruit trees which take up little space and look pretty too.

To avoid repeated descriptions of routine tasks such as sowing, thinning, feeding and picking, the key cultivation tasks are summarized for vegetables and fruit in extensive tables.

FRUIT & VEGETABLES

173

GROWING VEGETABLES AND HERBS

Make your kitchen garden as attractive and productive as possible through careful planning. If space is limited, try growing some of the more decorative vegetables and herbs in flower beds.

CHOOSING A SITE

Most fruits and vegetables need a sunny site to do well. Place fruit trees so they do not cast a shadow over the vegetables and plant herbs in a sunny place.

There's always space to grow a few herbs. Many make pretty container plants.

DISPLAYING HERBS

Many herbs are leafy and dull and a herb garden is a good way to display them. If it has a geometric shape, then it will be a feature even in winter. If you have the space, make it complex and ornate with a centrepiece such as a birdbath or sundial.

If you do not have space for a formal herb garden, a 'chequer-board' garden makes an interesting feature for a large patio.

Herbs are easy to integrate with flowers. Plants like thyme, shown here, and chives, make good edging for flower beds.

Most herbs do well in containers, and compact ornamental herbs are ideal.

Many herbs are decorative enough to grow in the flower border. Place tall ones at the back and use low-growing herbs as an edging.

WAYS WITH VEGETABLES

The conventional method of growing vegetables is in long rows.

Above A basketful of courgettes is just one of the regular delights for anyone who can find space for vegetables.

Opposite The kitchen garden can look attractive and be productive. The 1.2m (4ft) bed system has been used in this plot.

This is a convenient way to grow them, and if kept weeded, can look attractive too.

The 1.2m (4ft) bed system is popular with organic gardeners as the beds are wide enough for cultivation to be carried out easily from the paths on each side. This means you do not need to walk on the soil which can compact it. Mulching can prevent the need for digging. Spacing may need to be adjusted to allow room to walk between the rows.

A large range of vegetables can even be grown in containers—such as peas and potatoes.

Some vegetables are decorative enough to be among flowers, if you don't mind gaps once you begin to harvest them.

GROUNDWORK

A vegetable plot needs digging at least once a year, and deep digging is beneficial for some crops. Spend time thinking about crop rotation and planning what to plant where.

DOUBLE DIGGING

1 Start by digging out a trench 60cm (2ft) wide and barrowing the soil to the other end of the trench.

2 Fork over the bottom of the trench.

3 Spread a layer of manure or compost over the forked area.

4 Dig out the next trench, throwing the soil forward to fill the excavation left by the previous one. Fill the last trench with soil put to one side.

CATCH CROPS AND INTERCROPS

To make the best use of available space, grow quick-maturing crops between slower-growing ones. If you plant lettuces in the ground between sweet corn plants, they will keep the ground free of weeds and should be ready before the sweet corn casts too much shade. Radish seed mixed with parsnip seed, allows you to crop the radishes before the slower parsnips need all the space.

Catch cropping enables you to sneak in a quick crop in cleared ground. Early potatoes might allow you to plant a lettuce crop.

CROP ROTATION

By rotating the position of various types of crop you can reduce the risk of certain pests and diseases in the soil, and you can group crops with similar needs in terms of soil fertility and its pH level.

There are several variations, some people use a four-year rotation, but a three-year rotation is fine for a small garden or allotment.

One part is kept for perennial crops, the rest is divided up into three parts. Each year the crops are rotated within these three areas as shown.

GROUP A
Grow: aubergines, beetroot, carrots, celeriac, celery, courgettes, cucumber, garlic, leeks, marrows, onions, parsnips, peppers, potatoes, pumpkins, salsify, scorzonera, shallots, tomatoes.
Dig and feed: double dig, add manure, feed crops.

GROUP B
Grow: broad beans, chicory, French beans, lettuce, peas, runner beans, spinach, Swiss chard, sweet corn.
Dig and feed: single dig, apply fertilizer at start of the season, before sowing.

GROUP C
Grow: broccoli, Brussel sprouts, cabbages, cauliflowers, kale, kohl rabi, turnips, radishes, swedes.
Dig and feed: single dig, add lime if needed to bring the pH of the soil to 6.5–7.0. Apply a general fertilizer in the spring, and a supplement if needed during the season.

GROUP D
Grow: any crops that need to remain in the same piece of ground, such as asparagus, globe artichokes, rhubarb or Jerusalem artichokes.

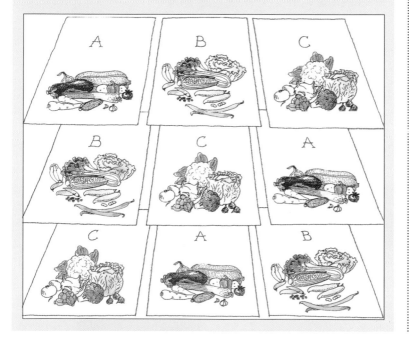

MANURES AND FERTILIZERS

Fruit and vegetables need plenty of feeding for good crops. Synthetic fertilizers are good for a short-term boost, but adding humus improves the soil structure as well as feeding the plants. This almost always leads to better crops than those grown only by the use of artificial fertilizers.

ADDING FERTILIZERS

1 A hopper is the most efficient way to distribute fertilizer to an allotment or large kitchen garden. Calculate the rate, then fill and simply push along the rows.

2 If applying by hand, measure the amount required for a square metre or yard. A small container can be marked with the quantity for easy spreading.

3 Mark off the area with strings stretched 1m (1yd) apart to divide the area into metre or yard squares.

4 Pour the fertilizer into your free hand and scatter as evenly as possible over the area. For each small square, use the container to scoop up the right quantity each time.

5 Rake the fertilizer into the surface before sowing or planting.

6 Some plants need a boost while growing. Cabbages benefit from nitrogenous fertilizer. Sprinkle it around the individual plants, keeping it off the leaves, then hoe or water in.

7 Most fruit trees will benefit from a general garden fertilizer in the spring. Sprinkle it around the base of the tree tree, keeping it off the trunk, then hoe it in.

MAKING GARDEN COMPOST

1 Compost bins are useful but you can save money in the kitchen garden by making a heap like this. Start with a thick layer of waste vegetable matter, 1m (1yd) square.

2 Tread the heap to compact the material when it is 30cm (1ft) deep, then sprinkle on sulphate of ammonia or a compost accelerator.

3 Continue to add garden or kitchen waste, with grass cuttings (not if weedkiller has recently been used on the lawn).

4 Continue to build up the heap in layers like this, and water if possible when the weather is dry.

5 After several months, depending on the time of year and the weather, the compost will be ready for use. Use any unrotted compost from around the edge to form the base for a new heap.

AN EARLY START 1

Cloches are the next best thing to a greenhouse or cold frame, and indispensable if you want fresh vegetables early or late in the season, when they are more expensive in the shops.

3 Right Plant out early vegetables that are hardy, such as broad beans or the hardiest of lettuces, once the ground has warmed up for a week or two. Make as much use of the space in a large cloche by sowing radishes or carrots either side of lettuces.

WARMING THE SOIL

1 In spring, put cloches in a couple of weeks before sowing to warm the ground.

2 Pay attention to the end pieces, or the cloche will become a wind tunnel. Ends can be a sheet of glass, but proprietary cloches have specially designed ends. Make sure the cloche is secured with pegs.

4 Right Tent cloches are less expensive, but as good for warming up the ground and protecting seedlings.

TUNNEL CLOCHES

1 Plastic tunnel cloches are useful for starting off early vegetable seedlings.

2 Make sure the plastic is secured with wires or strong wind will damage them.

3 Secure both ends firmly to resist the wind and pull the plastic taut.

FLEECY FILMS

1 Horticultural fleece will protect your crops from a degree or two of frost. Once the seedlings have been sown, pull over the fleece and secure with bricks.

2 Lay the fleece over the area so there is room for the crops to grow, but cover the edges with soil so no gaps are left. Water normally.

FLOATING CLOCHES

Protective netting give some protection against wind and hail and exclude many pests. They provide a little frost protection. Peel back the netting to weed or thin seedlings, replacing it later.
Perforated plastic film (right) will protect seedlings like other floating cloches and are long-lasting.

WHEN TO USE FLOATING CLOCHES

Floating cloches are used in the spring, but they can be useful for autumn protection too. Liquids will penetrate them, so you can water and apply liquid feeds through them. To weed or feed with non-liquid fertilizer, peel back the material and put it back when finished.

Many vegetables can be left under the cloche until they mature but not any which need pollinating, such as dwarf beans.

4 Use soil to hold down the edges of the cloche to stop the wind lifting them.

5 Use a soil thermometer to test if the soil is more than 7°C (45°F) for germination.

6 Either remove the cloche for sowing or planting or pull up the plastic on one side.

AN EARLY START 2

Many vegetables can be started off in pots or trays so that they are already growing well when you plant them out. You will be able to harvest them many weeks before those sown in open ground

Right Cabbages can be sown outdoors but also in pots indoors for an early start.

STARTING OFF SHALLOTS AND GARLIC

1 Start off large shallots in pots in a greenhouse or frame, in early winter. Plant so that the base of the bulb just sits in the loam-based compost or soil.

2 Keep moist. They will grow better in gentle warmth. Try to keep them growing slowly and in good light. Put in the garden 15–20cm (6–8in) apart in early spring.

3 Garlic is best planted in the garden in the autumn. They can be put into modules like these in mid or late winter, covered with 2.5cm (1in) of compost, planted out in the spring.

AN EARLY ROW OF PEAS

1 Sow peas in a piece of guttering lined with garden soil. Cover with more soil, put in the greenhouse in good light until they are 8cm (3in) tall.

2 Dig a wide drill the depth of the guttering. Use a garden line to make sure you keep the drill straight.

3 Slide the compost out of the length of gutter and into the drill. Firm the soil around the new row of peas, then cover with cloches to advance growth.

EARLY RUNNER BEANS

1 Eight weeks before the last frost is likely, sow runner bean seeds in pots, three to a pot. You can thin to two plants later.

2 Cover the seeds with 5cm (2in) of compost. Place in a light position in a frost-free greenhouse and keep watered.

3 Harden them off two weeks before planting out in a cold frame. Plant out when safe to do so.

SOWING IN POTS

1 Vegetables sown in pots can be given a good start. This is useful for brassicas if you have club-root disease in the soil. The plants will be better able to resist the disease with sterilized compost.

2 If more than one seedling germinates, thin to just one in each pot.

3 Once hardened off, plant them in the garden.

SOWING IN MODULES

1 These are useful for many types of vegetables, such as lettuce, that are planted out while still small. Sow a couple of seeds in each.

2 If more than one seed germinates, thin to one seedling while still small.

3 Make sure the seedlings have been watered before planting out, and remove each one with its root ball intact. They will grow quickly if planted this way.

EXTENDING THE SEASON

Use your cloches at the end
of the season as well as the
beginning, and protect your
vegetables for winter use.

WINTER PROTECTION

Right Some vegetables and
herbs, such as parsley, will continue to crop for much longer if
you cover the row with cloches
before cold weather arrives. Be
sure to cover each end, so that
the cloche does not become a
wind tunnel.

PROTECT FROM FROST

1 In mild areas
both beet-
root and celeri-
ac can be left
in the ground
for winter use if
the soil is well
drained. Protect
from severe
frosts with a
layer of straw
15cm (6in)
deep.

2 In cold areas, lift the vegetables, twist off the tops and
store in moist sand in a frost-
free place.

SOW WINTER SALADS

1 Extend fresh winter vegetables, by sowing winter radishes and corn salad (lamb's lettuce) in late summer.

2 They can be sown in the open, but do better in a cold frame with a cloche.

3 Winter radishes are sown in late summer. Lift the roots in late autumn to store in damp sand, in a cold dark place.

RIPEN LATE TOMATOES

Use cloches to ripen outdoor tomatoes at the end of the season. Lay straw on the ground, remove the supports and let the plants lie down on the straw.

Cover the row of cloches to speed the ripening process. Large barn cloches are best for this.

CORN SALAD

Sow corn salad (lamb's lettuce) in late summer. Harvest the leaves, a few at a time as needed.

ENCOURAGING FURTHER CROPPING

FRUIT & VEGETABLES

It may be possible for some crops to produce a bonus crop, even after harvesting.

EXTRA SPRING GREENS

Leave the stump after harvesting early cabbages. Make a cross-shaped cut i the stalk with a sharp knife. After a few weeks a cluster of small heads will have grown. Harvest these for a crop of spring greens.

MORE CALABRESE

Cut as normal, but do not discard the plant. Leave it to grow smaller heads on side shoots.

Harvest the smaller heads on side shoots, after a few weeks.

CUT-AND-COME-AGAIN LETTUCE

1 Loose-leaf lettuce can be harvested in stages. Remove leaves from several plants in the row.

2 If a whole head is needed, try harvesting by cutting across the plant 2.5cm (1in) above the soil. The stump should resprout for a second harvest.

HARVESTING SPINACH

1 Harvest ordinary and New Zealand spinach a few leaves at a time. The tips of New Zealand spinach as well as the leaves, to prevent flowering and produce side shoots.

2 When harvesting whole spinach plants try cutting the leaves 2.5cm (1in) above ground, as they will often regrow and produce another crop of leaves.

PAK CHOI AND CHINESE CABBAGES

Harvest your pak choi while they are still young. Cut off the leaves 2.5cm (1in) above the soil. New leaves will be produced for a later crop.

Harvest Chinese cabbages by cutting them off 2.5cm (1in) above the ground, leaving a stump. New growth will appear within a few weeks.

By growing a selection of different lettuce varieties, you will be able to harvest over a longer period...especially if you stagger the sowings. Include some loose-leaf varieties that you can harvest as individual leaves, often over a period of several months.

SOWING VEGETABLES 1

FRUIT & VEGETABLES

Get your vegetables off to a good start by preparing the seed beds carefully

PREPARING THE GROUND

1 Break down clods of soil left after rough digging, to produce a fine surface for sowing.

2 If large lumps are difficult to break down, try treading on them to crumble them into smaller pieces.

3 Rake the soil level, gathering any large stones to one end.

4 Leave small stones, but remove large ones.

SOW WINTER SALADS

1 Always use a garden line to keep the rows straight. Wind the surplus around a peg keeping the line taut.

2 Use the corner of a hoe or rake to make a drill. Try to keep to the recommended depth on the packet.

3 Sprinkle the seeds thinly, and as evenly as possible. If this is difficult buy a seed dispenser.

Most gardeners sow vegetables in long rows, but use a 1.2m (4ft) bed system and you avoid treading on the ground to weed, cultivate and harvest, as you can reach the rows from both sides. If you mulch well, this can be the basis of a no-dig method of cultivation as the soil is not compacted.

The rows can be sown closer together with this method.

4 If dry, run water into the drill first to soak the soil. Water before sowing to reduce the chance of seeds being washed away.

5 Cover the seeds by shuffling your feet along the sides of the drill, pushing the soil back into the drills.

6 You may find it easier to rake the soil back into the drill, but be careful to rake in the direction of the drill and not across it.

SOWING VEGETABLES 2

Although most vegetables are best sown in convention-al single rows, some can be sown broadcast, and others are best sown in multiple rows. Consider fluid sowing where you need to get tricky crops of to an early start.

Closer spacing is possible if you grow your vegetables in 1.2m (4ft) beds. Traditional row spacings allow for having to walk between the plants from routine cultiva-tion.

SOWING MULTIPLE ROWS

1 Some seeds are usually sown in multiple rows close togeth-er. Take out a wide drill with a draw hoe.

2 Space the seed in the bottom of the drill. Large seeds like peas and beans can be spaced accurately by hand.

3 Push the soil back. Cover with mesh wire-netting if mice and birds are a problem until the seeds germinate

FLUID SOWING

1 Fluid sowing gets seeds off to a good start. Use it for parsnips and parsley. Sow thickly onto damp kitchen paper. Keep in a warm place.

2 Check daily and keep moist. As soon as roots emerge, wash them off the paper into a sieve. Don't wait for leaves to grow.

3 Mix wallpaper paste without fungicide, or use a kit from a garden centre. Stir the seeds into the paste to mix them well.

4 Take out the drill as you would normally, at the usual depth.

5 Place the paste in a plastic bag and cut off one corner. Do not make the hole too big. Twist the top of the bag and squeeze the paste along the drill. Cover with soil and water if dry.

SOWING BROADCAST

1 Some seeds can be sown broadcast. Scatter as evenly as possible on prepared ground.

2 Rake the seeds into the soil, in the opposite direction to when the ground was prepared, to distribute the seeds better.

THINNING AND TRANSPLANTING

Thin your vegetables while they are still small, so that you have a full row of well-spaced plants. Take special care with vegetables which need to be transplanted.

MULTIPLE SOWING

Some growers plant out vegetables in small clusters of seedlings, such as carrots, onions and leeks.

They are best grown in modules of four to six seeds in a cell.

Plant out intact, without separating them. You will not get exhibition quality crops but the overall weight is often good.

BEWARE CARROT FLY

Carrot flies lay their eggs around carrots when they are thinned. The smell of crushed leaves is thought to attract them.

Thin in the evening. Nip the surplus plants off at ground level, do not pull up.

Take the thinnings away with you, rather than leaving them on the ground.

THINNING

1 Thin as soon as seedlings are large enough to handle. Leave remaining seedlings twice as close as the final spacing to allow for losses.

2 When the seedlings are almost touching, thin to their final spacing. If there are gaps it may be possible to lift some of the thinnings carefully and transplant to make good the gaps.

TRANSPLANTING

1 When transplanting from open ground, water thoroughly an hour before, if the weather is dry.

2 Loosen the soil if plants are close together, or lift with a hand fork so that each seedling has a ball of soil attached.

3 Plant out with a trowel, firming the soil as you go. Use the blade of the trowel to press the soil around the roots.

4 The handle of the trowel can be used instead but the trowel will get dirty and unpleasant to use.

192

PLANTING OUT FROM MODULES, TRAYS AND POTS

1 The compost must be moist before removing the seedlings from the trays. To remove them, squeeze out from the base, while gently pulling at the top.

2 A plant grown in a pot will come out cleanly if you invert the pot. Hold the plant between your fingers and shake gently. Tapping the bottom of the pot will remove any stuck plants.

3 Plant the seedlings with a trowel, at their final spacing, then firm the soil gently and water in well

PLANTING BRASSICAS

1 If club root is a problem, grow your brassica seedlings in pots of sterilized compost and plant out when they're growing strongly. This will not eliminate the disease but the plants get off to a good start and the effects will be minimized.

2 Brassicas are also attacked by cabbage root fly, the larvae burrow into the roots and stems. Place a proprietary or improvised brassica collar around each seedling, making sure that it lies flat on the soil. This will deter the flies.

STAKING AND SUPPORTING

Runner and climbing French beans, tall peas and tomatoes all need some form of support, which should be inserted when the plants are small.

GROWING BAG SUPPORTS

This is just of one the types of support for canes in growing bags. They hold the canes upright in the shallow compost. They are expensive but will last for many years.

PEA STICKS

Save twiggy sticks from prunings or cut from a tree. Select the right height for the plant and push the stick into the ground between the peas when they are 5cm (2in) high. The peas support themselves by curling tendrils around the sticks.

NETTING

Nylon netting is a good support for both peas and beans. Stretch it between two posts or make a framework from battens or canes. Use a 10cm (4in) mesh and tie it on securely. Young beans may need to be threaded through to start them climbing.

BAMBOO CANES

1 A wigwam of canes is ideal for a few runner bean plants and will look attractive at the back of the border. Tie four to six canes together near the top or use a plastic holder which the canes are pushed through.

2 Runner beans will twine around the canes and be self-clinging. Start them off by winding them round the canes, keeping them off the soil where they are vulnerable to slug and snail damage.

3 For a long row of runner or climbing French beans, insert two rows of 2.4m (8ft) canes at a slight angle so they cross near the top.

4 Slide a horizontal cane along the top in the V formed by the crossed canes. Pull it downwards to wedge the canes, then tie them all together.

5 Individual canes are useful for tomatoes, but make sure that 30–60cm (1–2ft) of the cane is pushed into the ground, to support the weight of a fruiting plant.

ROUTINE CARE

Regular weeding, feeding and watering will bring out the best in your vegetables. The increased yields always make the effort worthwhile.

WEEDING

1 Regular hoeing is the best way to keep down the weeds. A Dutch hoe is the most efficient, but can be difficult to manoeuvre between close plants.

2 Hand-weeding is inevitable if the weeds grow close to the crops plants. Pull up the weed with one hand while holding the vegetable firmly to reduce root disturbance.

3 Pernicious weeds, such as thistles and bindweed, will break off if they are pulled and spread further. If you are careful, you can paint translocated weedkiller on to the leaves, killing the roots. Be careful not to touch the crop plants.

FEEDING

1 A balanced fertilizer should be applied before planting. Some vegetables benefit from a specific fertilizer as the season progresses. Sprinkle it along the rows at the recommended rate, keeping it off leaves.

2 Use liquid fertilizers to boost growth during the summer. Most plants will usually respond rapidly to a liquid feed at this time. Dilute according to instructions.

WATERING

Sprinkler The best way to water a vegetable garden is with a sprinkler that distributes the water over a wide area.
Seep hose (right) are effective for vegetables planted in rows.
Once one row has been watered thoroughly, move the hose to the next one.

SPECIAL TECHNIQUES 1

Some vegetables, such as chicory and endive, are more succulent and less bitter if you blanch them. Rhubarb is forced in the dark to provide tender young stems earlier than normal.

GROWING AND FORCING CHICORY

1 To produce chicons (blanched heads) for winter use, sow in late spring or early summer. Lift the roots from mid-autumn onwards, and leave them exposed for a couple of days to retard growth.

2 When the roots have dried, trim off the leaves 2.5–5cm (1–2in) above the top of the root. Store any spare roots in a box of sand, peat or dry soil, until you are ready to use them.

3 Right Trim the bottom of each root so that it fits a 15–23cm (6–9in) pot. Pack soil around the roots, so the shoulder of each root is just beneath the soil. Put a pot of the same size over the top, and cover the holes. Keep in a temperature of 10°C (50°F) for 3 weeks, keeping moist, and harvest when they are 15cm (6in) tall.

FORCING RHUBARB

1 To force rhubarb in the garden, place an old barrel or wooden box over a root in early to mid winter, or use wire netting and canes as shown.

2 A better crop will result if straw is piled into the cage to generate warmth. With a wooden box, pile manure over the top and around the sides.

3 A plastic dustbin with the bottom cut out can be used. Check growth after a couple of months, pulling stems when they are 25–30cm (10–12in) long.

4 Roots can be forced indoors, but first lift a crown at least two years old and exposed to the cold for a few weeks. Put the crown in a black plastic sack and pack slightly moist peat or soil around the root or pot it up. If too wet, the soil will encourage fungus diseases. Secure the top with a twist-tie.

5 Place the sack in a warm place indoors until the forced stems are ready to harvest. Discard any roots or stems with fungus.

BLANCHING ENDIVE

Grow endive as lettuce, but blanch the leaves so they are not too bitter. Two weeks before harvesting, cover each plant with an old plate or blanching dish sold especially for the purpose.

Remove the cover only when you are ready to eat the endive. The covered area will be pale and less bitter.

Far right Rhubarb is so easy to grow that it is often taken for granted. It makes a decorative foliage plant and the forced stems are an early treat.

SPECIAL TECHNIQUES 2

Tomatoes can be grown well outdoors if you choose a suitable variety. In cold areas try raising tomatoes in grow bags or pots in a porch. If you have been put off growing potatoes because of the hard work earthing and lifting up, try growing them under black polythene.

POTATOES UNDER POLYTHENE

1 Roll out the polythene over the prepared ground. To prevent the polythene being blown away, pull soil over the edges to secure it in place.

2 Make slits in the polythene, spaced for the variety you intend to grow. Plants the tubers through the slits with a trowel

CHITTING

If you chit the tubers you will have a crop several weeks earlier.

Place the potatoes in trays in a frost-free place. The tubers are ready to plant when they are 2cm ($3/4$in) long.

3 Once the tops have died down, harvest the potatoes by lifting the polythene. Most of the potatoes will be lying on the surface ready to harvest.

EARTHING UP

Potatoes grown in the ground have to be earthed up to prevent the tubers being exposed to the light. This can cause them to turn green and become inedible.

Earth up in stages using a hoe to mound soil up each side of the plants.

OUTDOOR TOMATOES

1 Plant tall varieties that need staking 38–45cm (15–18in) apart, once hardened off.

2 Protect the plants with a barn cloche initially, to get them off to a good start.

GROWING BAGS AND POTS

Tomatoes do well in growing bags, using special supports makes staking easy. You can also grow bush types if you do not want to stake.

If a heavy crop is not essential, grow suitable varieties in pots.

3 When the plants are too tall for the cloches, remove them and stake immediately. Use one stake for each plant and push them well into the ground.

4 Keep the main stem tied to the support as it grows. Remove all sideshoots by pinching out the growing tips. Let the plant concentrate on the lower trusses of fruit.

5 Bush and dwarf tomatoes sprawl on the ground and do not need staking. Plant them 30–75cm (12–30in) apart. Cover with a floating cloche, if possible, until harvesting or they grow too tall.

SPECIAL TECHNIQUES 3

FRUIT & VEGETABLES

Traditional trench varieties of celery require blanching, but you can grow the self-blanching type in blocks and let them blanch each other. Carrots can be an easy crop to grow, but if carrot fly usually devastates your crop beat it with a simple barrier.

BEATING CARROT FLY

Erect a barrier of polythene or mesh netting around vulnerable seedlings, if carrot fly is a problem. Chemicals have limited success.

Make the barrier 60–90cm (2–3ft) high, beyond the height the fly normally reaches.

SELF-BLANCHING CELERY

1 Plant self-blanching varieties in blocks rather than rows. The inner plants are then protected by the outer ones. Plant celery 23cm (9in) apart to increase the blanching effect.

2 Harvest by lifting with a fork. You will have to discard more leaves from the heads on the outside of the block than in the inner part.

BLANCHING TRENCH CELERY

1 Trench varieties are usually planted in a trench to make blanching and watering easier. Fork in as much organic matter and manure, as possible.

2 Plant in rows 30cm (12in) apart, with 25cm (10in) between the plants.

3 Keep well watered. The trench can easily be flooded with water periodically in dry weather.

4 Some people earth up their celery with soil, but many gardeners prefer to blanch the stems with paper or drainpipes. Wrap corrugated cardboard or light paper loosely around the stems. Add more layers as the plants grow taller, overlapping the layers slightly.

SPECIAL TECHNIQUES 4

POLLINATING MARROWS AND COURGETTES

1 Marrows and courgettes are usually pollinated by insects, but hand pollination may be needed if the weather is cold or fruits are not forming. The female flower (left) has the small swelling, which is the embryonic fruit, behind the flower.

2 Pollinate marrows or courgettes with a fully open male flower, pressed against the female stigma.

3 A paintbrush can gather pollen from the male flower, then be brushed on to the stigma of the female.

4 Harvest courgettes while they are still young. The more you pick, the more fruits the plant will produce.

GROWING ONIONS FROM SETS

1 Make shallow drills 30cm (12in) apart. Space onion sets 15cm (6in) apart. Press firmly into the soil so the tips will protrude above the soil.

2 Cover the drills with soil so the tips of the onions are just visible. If birds pull at the onions, protect them until they form roots. Wire-netting or black cotton strung between pegs will deter the birds.

ENSURING SWEET CORN POLLINATION

1 Sweet-corn is wind-pollinated, and has male and female flowers. Male flowers are on top of the plant, females are below and form the cobs.

2 Block planting rather than in rows, will increase the chances of fertile cobs.

3 Press a fingernail into a kernel to test if it is ready to harvest. If milky liquid oozes out, the cob is ready. If the liquid looks watery, it is under-ripe.

Vegetables such as onions and courgettes are easy to grow, especially if you plant onion sets.

GREENHOUSE VEGETABLES 1: TOMATOES

Tomatoes are a popular greenhouse crop, and you should be able to harvest them over a long season. If you have a heated greenhouse start them early, if not, do not plant until you are sure there is no possibility of frost.

TOMATOES IN BORDERS

1 Right Try tomatoes in the greenhouse border for a couple of years. After that, replace the soil every two years, or use one of the other methods described. This will avoid problems from soil-borne pests and diseases. Plant 45cm (18in) apart from late winter in a heated greenhouse, or late spring in an unheated greenhouse. Tomatoes need regular feeding, use specially formulated liquid tomato feed for best results.

TOMATOES IN BORDERS

1 Ring culture is worth considering once the border ceases to be productive. Take out a trench and line with polythene to eliminate disease from the soil below.

2 Place fine gravel or coarse grit in the lined trench, and put special ring culture bottomless pots on top.

3 Fill the pots with good loam-based compost and plant the tomatoes. Water into the rings until roots are established, then water into the aggregate.

2 Although canes can be used for support, string is a more economical method.

3 As the plants grow, gently loop the string around the growing tip, to form a spiral.

4 Remove side and base-shoots while they are still small, by snapping off cleanly.

5 If fruits are failing to form shaking the plants each day and misting the flowers with water can help to spread the pollen.

6 Remove yellowing lower leaves. They are not needed and removing them will allow more light to reach the fruits.

7 Harvest the fruit when it is just ripe, and pick with the green calyx attached.

8 Right When six or seven sprays of fruit have set, remove the growing tip two leaves above the top spray of flowers, to allow these fruits to mature.

GROWING BAGS

1 These provide an alternative to a contaminated border, but careful watering and feeding are needed. Plant three tomatoes in a standard bag.

2 Cane supports can be pushed through the bottom of the bag into the border below, or strings can be suspended from the roof (see Tomatoes in Borders).

BUSH VARIETIES

The advice given above is for cordon or indeterminate varieties. Bush varieties are not normally grown in the greenhouse, but if they are, support will not be needed and sideshoots should not be pinched out.

GREENHOUSE VEGETABLES 2: AUBERGINES, CUCUMBERS, MELONS AND SWEET PEPPERS

All these vegetables are easy to grow in a greenhouse, and make a change from tomatoes. It is sometimes recommended that you avoid growing these different crops together, but in an amateur greenhouse, you can grow any combination of them.

Below Aubergines are decorative plants, and make a change from tomatoes in your greenhouse.

AUBERGINES

1 Aubergines can be grown in growing bags or 20cm (8in) pots with a loam-based compost. Pinch out the growing tip when the plant is 30cm (12in) tall.

2 Allow only one fruit to develop on each shoot. Remove other flowers and pinch out the growing tips, three leaves beyond the developing fruit.

3 The plants should be kept well watered and fed, and benefit from high humidity.

4 Fruits are heavy, so stake tall varieties. Purple fruits are usual although some are white. Harvest with at least 2.5cm (1in) of stalk attached.

CUCUMBERS

1 Bush varieties can be allowed to sprawl, but most greenhouse varieties are trained to wires or canes. Plant in growing bags or the border—two in a standard bag. One cane for each plant with wires stretched horizontally.

2 Tie the main stem to the cane. Pinch out the growing tip when it reaches the roof.

3 Many modern varieties produce only female flowers which have a small embryo fruit behind the petals.

4 Tie sideshoots to the wires. When tiny cucumbers grow, pinch out the shoots beyond two leaves after the fruit. Feed and water well, keep the air humid.

SWEET PEPPERS

Grow sweet peppers as described for aubergines, in pots or growing bags. Provide a stake, and pinch out the growing tip once the plants reach 60cm (2ft).

MELONS

1 Plant in a cool or heated greenhouse in late May, in growing bags or the border. Use a cane per plant, stretching wires horizontally across.

2 Tie the sideshoots to the wires. Pinch out the tip of the plant when it reaches 1.8m (6ft)

Pinch back all sideshoots on melon plants to two leaves beyond each flower. If necessary, pollinate by hand using a paintbrush. Thin to four fruits on each plant and support them in net slings.

PATIO VEGETABLES

You can grow a wide selection of vegetables in small spaces. Some are attractive enough in containers to make pleasant patio plants.

GROWING BAGS

1 These can be used for many vegetables, even early potatoes. Do not open the bag in the usual way, cut slits to plant the tubers through—equivalent to planting beneath black polythene.

2 Keep the plants well watered and feed with a liquid fertilizer.

3 One growing bag can produce a good crop of potatoes and be fun in the process.

4 Spinach and self-blanching celery can be grown in this way. Sow directly into the bag or plant as seedlings.

5 Peas and dwarf French beans can be sown directly into the bag.

6 **Right** Lettuce, salad onions and tomatoes can crop well in growing bags.

WINDOW BOXES

1 Miniature or tumbling varieties of tomatoes can be grown in windowboxes and even hanging baskets.

2 Cut-and-come-again varieties of lettuce can be grown in windowboxes. Just pick enough leaves for one meal at a time, taking care not to strip any plant totally.

TUBS AND POTS

1 Some varieties of tomato can be planted in pots or tubs. Plant in late spring or early summer, protect from late frosts. Feed regularly using liquid feed or slow-release fertilizer in the compost.

2 Compact varieties supply a good crop of tomatoes.

3 Courgettes and bush cucumbers do well in tubs or large pots, and can look very attractive too.

HARVESTING AND STORING

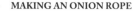

Correct harvesting and storage will enable you to enjoy the fruits of your labour, throughout the winter months.

MAKING AN ONION ROPE

1 Onions can be stored in nets, but an onion rope is attractive if the onions have been harvested with their dried stems intact.

2 Tie onions to the rope wrapping twine around the neck of each onion and the rope.

3 Hang the ropes in a cool place where air circulates freely around them.

PROTECTING CAULIFLOWER CURDS

If left unprotected, cauliflower curds discolour in the summer light and are damaged by frost in winter. Fold over the leaves to protect them.

When the curd is almost mature, fold over leaves to protect it. Bend them so they do not break, and the head will last in good condition for longer.

In winter, tie the outer leaves with string to hold them over the curd. This is important with older varieties, new varieties have leaves that curl anyway.

PICKING BRUSSELS SPROUTS

Varieties bred for freezing have sprouts that mature at about the same time. Others usually mature in succession. Pick the lowest ones first, leaving the smaller ones at the top to mature. Snap off any yellowing leaves to reduce the risk of disease.

FRUIT & VEGETABLES

STORING CARROTS AND BEETROOT

1 Lift any crops which you are unable to use to stop them rotting in the ground.

2 Twist off leaves or the roots may rot.

3 In a large box, lay the roots on damp sand so they do not touch each other. Build up layer by layer, finish with 15cm (6in) of soil or sand. Store in a cool shed or outside as shown.

STORING POTATOES

1 Lift potatoes for storing after the foliage has died down.

Below Store what you can for winter use.

2 Leave them on the surface for a couple of hours to dry.

3 Sort out the tubers, discarding the smallest, use up the middle-sized ones, and only store the largest. They must be kept frost-free, in paper sacks in a cool place. The potatoes must be dry before storing.

STORING WINTER CABBAGES

Winter white cabbage and red cabbages are best harvested while in good condition, and stored in a cool, frost-free place. Strip off the coarse outer leaves before storing.

Store them in a well-ventilated, cool place, just above freezing. Place them on a slatted bench (straw

will help to protect them, but it's not essential) or hang them in nets.

VEGETABLE FACTS AT YOUR FINGERTIPS

This table is a quick reference guide for advice on how to grow common vegetables. Always check the seed packet or planting instructions for dates and spacings.

VEGETABLE	SOW	PLANT	HARVEST
ARTICHOKE, GLOBE	Mid/late spring	Spring	Early summer to mid autumn
ARTICHOKE, JERUSALEM	Plant tubers	Early/mid spring	Mid summer to following spring
ASPARAGUS	Early/mid spring	Spring	Late spring
AUBERGINE	Late winter/early spring	Early summer	Late summer/early autumn
BEAN, BROAD	Spring or early autumn	Sow *in situ*	Summer
BEAN, FRENCH	Late Spring/early summer	Sow *in situ*	Summer
BEAN, RUNNER	Late Spring/early summer	Early summer	Summer
BEETROOT	Late Spring to mid summer	Sow *in situ*	Summer and autumn
BROCCOLI, SPROUTING	Mid/late spring	Spring	Late winter to mid spring
BRUSSELS SPROUT	Late winter to mid spring	Spring	Late summer/early winter
CABBAGE, CHINESE	Late Spring to mid summer	Summer	Summer and autumn
CABBAGE, SPRING	Late summer	Autumn	Spring
CABBAGE, SUMMER/ AUTUMN	Early to late spring	Spring/summer	Summer/autumn

VEGETABLE	SOW	PLANT	HARVEST
CABBAGE, WINTER	Spring	Late spring/summer	Winter
CALABRESE	Late winter to late spring	Sow *in situ*	Early summer to mid autumn
CAPSICUM	Late winter to early spring	Early summer	Mid summer to mid autumn
CARROT	Early spring to early summer	Sow *in situ*	Mid summer to mid autumn
CAULIFLOWER, EARLY SUMMER	Autumn or late winter (under glass)	Spring	Early summer
CAULIFLOWER, SUMMER/AUTUMN	Mid to late spring	Early summer	Summer and autumn
CAULIFLOWER, WINTER	Late spring	Summer	Winter (mild areas) or spring
CELERIAC	Early/mid spring	Late spring	Early/mid autumn
CELERY	Early/mid spring	Late spring	Late summer to late autumn
CHICORY, FOR CHICONS	Late spring/early summer	Sow *in situ*	Winter
CHICORY, HEARTING TYPE	Summer	Sow *in situ*	Autumn
CORN SALAD (LAMB'S LETTUCE)	Spring to autumn	Sow *in situ*	Summer, autumn, winter
CUCUMBER, INDOOR	Late winter to late spring	Spring or early summer	Summer to mid autumn
CUCUMBER, OUTDOOR	Late spring/early summer	Late spring or early summer	Summer

VEGETABLE	SOW	PLANT	HARVEST
ENDIVE	Mid spring to mid summer	Sow *in situ*	Mid summer to late autumn
KALE	Mid or late spring	Late spring or early summer	Autumn and winter
KOHL RABI	Early spring to early summer	Sow *in situ*	Early summer to mid autumn
LEEK	Mid winter to mid spring	Late spring or early summer	Mid autumn to early spring
LETTUCE	Early spring to mid summer	Late spring to mid summer	Early summer to mid autumn
MARROW, PUMPKIN, SQUASH, COURGETTE	Mid or late spring	Late spring or early summer	Mid summer to mid autumn
MELON	Late winter/early	Late spring/early spring	Mid summer to mid autumn
ONION	Late winter to mid spring	Early/mid spring	Mid summer to mid autumn
ONION, JAPANESE	Mid summer to early autumn	Sow *in situ*	Early spring to mid summer
ONION, SPRING OR BUNCHING	Early spring to early autumn	Sow *in situ*	Late spring to late autumn
PARSNIP	Late winter to mid spring	Sow *in situ*	Mid autumn to late winter
PEA	Early spring to early summer	Sow *in situ*	Summer
POTATO	Plant tubers	Mid or late spring	Early summer to late summer

VEGETABLE	SOW	PLANT	HARVEST
RADISH	Early spring to early autumn	Sow *in situ*	Mid spring to late autumn
RADISH, WINTER	Mid summer to mid autumn	Sow *in situ*	Mid autumn to early winter
SALSIFY	Early to late spring	Sow *in situ*	Mid autumn to late winter
SCORZONERA	Mid/late spring	Sow *in situ*	Mid autumn to early spring
SHALLOT	Plant sets (bulbs)	Late winter to mid spring	Mid summer to early autumn
SPINACH	Late winter to mid summer	Sow *in situ*	Late spring to mid autumn
SPINACH, NEW ZEALAND	Spring	Sow *in situ*	Mid summer to mid autumn
SWEDE	Late spring/early summer	Sow *in situ*	Mid autumn to early spring
SWEET CORN	Mid/late spring	Late spring/early summer	Late summer/early autumn
SWISS CHARD	Early spring to mid summer	Sow *in situ*	Mid summer to mid autumn
TOMATO, INDOOR	Mid winter to early spring	Early to late spring	Early summer to mid autumn
TOMATO, OUTDOOR	Early to mid spring	Late spring/early summer	Mid summer to mid autumn
TURNIP	Early spring to early summer	Sow *in situ*	Early summer to mid autumn

GROWING HERBS

Few gardeners have space for a formal herb garden, but a mini herb garden is possible in a small space. Some ornamental herbs can be grown in flower beds and borders.

MAKING A HERB WHEEL

1 A herb wheel is a feature which allows you to grow a small collection of herbs. An old cartwheel could have herbs planted between the spokes.

A brick version can be made using a circle with a diameter of 1.5m (5ft) or larger. If there is space, plant an upright rosemary in the centre.

2 Lay a circle of bricks on end or at an angle to create a dog-tooth effect. Adjust the diameter of the circle if necessary for a close fit. The bricks can be laid on a shallow mortar base. When set, mortar the bricks in place. Otherwise, compact the soil around each brick, checking levels with a spirit-level.

3 Lay lines of bricks as the 'spokes', leaving plenty of room for planting. If the bricks do not meet exactly in the centre, do not worry. Mask any gaps with a plant or ornament—or an attractive pot containing herbs.

4 Top up the soil between the spokes with a loam-based potting compost, or good garden soil.

5 Plant up your herb wheel with a collection of perennial herbs that you will use and that are ornamental.

6 Finish off, by covering surface with stone chippings or cocoa shells.

PLANNING FOR WINTER

1 Pot up a few herbs that are small enough and that will grow on indoors. Chives can be treated this way.

2 Plant up in 15–20cm (6–8in) pots, water well and keep by a light window.

3 Lift some mint before it dies back in autumn. Pot up in and keep on a light window-sill.

HERBS IN CONTAINERS

FRUIT & VEGETABLES a

Containers offer plenty of scope when space is limited, or if you want herbs by the back door or on a patio.

GROWING BAGS

1 Mint does well in a growing bag, and this ensures that it does not invade the rest of the garden. Different mints can be grown together in one bag, four at a time, and can be harvested as you need.

2 Growing bags are suitable for many low-growing annual herbs.

PLANTING A BARREL OR TUB

1 Use a large container for shrubby herbs such as bay. Drainage holes should be clear and use a loam-based compost.

2 If the plant is small for the container, plant a decorative edging of a compact herb such as golden thyme.

PLANTING A HERB POT

1 Herb pots look attractive, but always bear in mind the ultimate size and spread of each herb. Put small herbs in the planting pockets. Fill the pot with compost to that level, add the roots, then add more compost. Plant an attractive shallow-rooting herb in the top.

2 A herb pot like this is a very decorative feature, so harvest just a few leaves at a time, to avoid spoiling the effect.

WINDOWBOXES

Herbs can make attractive windowbox plants, using compact types such as marjorams, parsley and mints. Shrubby sage can be used but be prepared to replant every year or so.

HARVESTING AND STORING HERBS

Herbs are best harvested fresh, but many can be dried or preserved in other ways to enjoy when fresh herbs are not available.

COLLECTING FRESH HERBS

1 Herbs such as basil, tarragon and marjoram should have the growing tips used first. Harvest the larger leaves later.

2 Pick the outer leaves from parsley, sorrel, lovage and salad burnet first. More leaves will continue to grow.

3 Harvest leaves and sprigs from shrubby herbs, such as rosemary and thyme from areas that do not spoil the shape.

4 Harvest chives and Welsh onions by cutting them down to 4cm (1.5in) with scissors. More leaves will grow back.

Although most herbs are best used fresh, as soon as possible after picking, most can be dried or frozen.

AIR DRYING

1 Hang those herbs that can be cut as sprigs to dry in an airy place. Tie them in small bunches and they will be dry enough after a week.

2 Dry leaves on a wire rack. For small leaves, cover the rack with muslin or cheesecloth. Do not wash the leaves, but wipe off any dirt. Leave them in a dark place for a week.

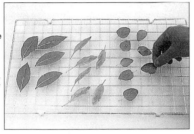

3 Store in glass bottles (dark glass is best). Plastic and metal containers can affect the chemistry of some herbs. Label carefully.

FREEZING

1 Many herbs can be frozen. Chopped parsley, chives, and mint all freeze well. Use equal measures of water and chopped herbs. Whole leaves can be put into trays of water.

2 Whole sprigs can be put in the freezer and crumble easily when frozen. Blanch and dry first, if storing for a long time.

GROWING FRUIT

To grow a wide variety of fruit you do not need an orchard or very large garden Small apple trees grow in patio pots, strawberries grow well in containers on a balcony, and cordon trained apples and pears look good against a garden fence.

CHOOSING A SITE

Almost all fruits prefer a sunny site, avoiding frost pockets and cold air.

You will suffer poor crops if frost damages the blossom on tress like apples and pears. The latter are vulnerable as they flower earlier than apples. In a mixed kitchen garden, plant fruit trees so they do not cast shadows over the vegetables.

FRUITFUL IDEAS

If space is small, plant trained fruit trees, such as fans, cordons or espaliers,

against a wall or fence. They look decorative and take up little room.

Ballerina apple trees grow as a narrow column, even without pruning, and make an ornamental feature both in flower and fruit.

Some fruits can be grown well in tubs or pots on the patio where they will make a feature. Apple trees should have been grafted to a very dwarfing rootstock. Avoid vigorous trees such as pears.

You can even grow an apple as a decorative edging to a bed, perhaps in the kitchen garden. Step-over apples are single-armed espaliers.

The step-over method (left) makes an ornamental edging. 'Ballerina' apples (bottom of opposite page) grow into narrow columns.

Even rampant fruits like blackberries, as well as hybrid berries, can be trained to look neat. They won't become overgrown, or be difficult to pick at harvest time, if they are trained to wires stretched between stout posts.

Apples pruned like cordons can be trained over a strong arch instead of against angled canes. Don't try hazardous thorned fruit.

PLANTING A FRUIT TREE OR BUSH 1

Fruit trees will be in the ground for a long time, so thorough ground preparation is vital. Plant with care.

PLANTING A CORDON OR ESPALIER

1 Fix the horizontal wires first, spacing them 30–45cm (12–18in) apart, and 10–15cm (4–6in) away from the fence or wall. Secure a cane at an angle of 45°, if planting a cordon.

2 Plant the tree with the stem 23cm (9in) away from the wall or fence. Place a cane across the hole to check levels. If planting a cordon, make sure that the stem can be tied to the cane.

PLANTING A FREE-STANDING TREE

1 Make a hole one-third larger than the width of the tree container. Add manure or compost and fork over so the plant does not sit on compacted ground.

2 Test the root ball for size and depth. Adjust soil levels if needed. If adding a stake, do this now, on one side of the hole, before you plant the tree.

3 Tease out some of the roots to encourage them to grow out. Return the soil, enriching it with compost, manure or slow-release fertilizer if necessary.

4 Tread the soil firmly with your feet to remove any air pockets.

5 Hoe the firmed soil to remove your footprints, and mulch the surface to conserve moisture and suppress weeds.

1 Prepare the ground as for trees, making the hole wider than the root ball. Use a cane to check levels.

3 Mix a slow-release fertilizer into the soil. Rake level, firm with your feet and water well.

Below Every garden has some space for fruit—a cordon pear can be trained against a fence.

4 If planting a cordon, tie the stem to the oblique cane in several places to ensure it grows at the correct angle. Tie the main stem upright of an espalier, securing horizontal branches to the wires.

2 Hoe and rake the ground to remove weeds and compressed footprints.

3 Cut back hard those bushes which grow on stems that sprout from a low base.

PLANTING A BARE-ROOTED TREE

Spread the roots out as widely as possible in the planting hole. Enlarge the hole if necessary.

FRUIT & VEGETABLES

PLANTING A FRUIT TREE 2

FRUIT & VEGETABLES

Trees need staking initially, but using an inappropriate tree tie can do more harm than good. In exposed gardens, or for very large trees, a different staking method may be used. The examples here are adequate for the majority of ordinary garden trees.

STAKING A FRUIT TREE

1 A low stake is better than a tall one, as the flexing of the stem in the wind can help to strengthen it. Insert the stake when planting, so at least 60cm (2ft) should be in the ground.

2 Use a proprietary tree tie as they are easy to adjust and have a spacer to hold the stem away from the tree.

ROOTSTOCKS

The rootstock determines the vigour and size of your fruit tree. Trained trees will almost certainly have been grafted on to an appropriate rootstock by the nursery. For bush and standard trees, you need to make sure that you select one with an appropriate rootstock.

The illustration shows the relative heights for an apple tree of the same age on different rootstocks. They indicate the space needed to grow them.

A dwarfing rootstock is useful for cherries and plums if you have a small garden. The cherry rootstock called 'Colt', for example, will

reduce the tree's size by about one-third (and it will crop sooner). Most plums sold in garden centres will have been grafted on to a dwarfing rootstock.

The rootstocks available vary in different countries, so if in doubt ask about the characteristics of the rootstock before you buy.

These are the likely heights of apples grown on different rootstocks. The more dwarfing the rootstock, the lighter the crop will be. The tree will fruit sooner and it may be possible to grow fruit in a garden that would otherwise be too small.

3 Make sure the tree is held firmly against the spacer.

4 Check ties every year, loosening when the trunk has expanded. Staking is needed for about the first three years.

Above Most fruits trees benefit from initial staking, especially those grown on very dwarfing rootstocks. Always check the ties annually as they may need to be loosened to prevent the ties biting into the stem.

5 Use a mulch, at least 5cm (2in) thick to suppress weeds and conserve moisture. Chipped bark is long-lasting and looks good.

6 Use a tree guard to protect the trunk if rabbits are a problem, stripping off the bark.

PRUNING TRAINED APPLES AND PEARS

Intensively trained apples and pears, grown as cordon and espaliers, must be pruned in summer and winter, to encourage cropping.

Opposite Apples and pears trained against a wall or fence can look very attractive. This is an espalier-trained pear: the pretty blossom will be followed by a heavy crop of tasty fruit.

PRUNING A CORDON

1 Shorten any long shoots grown since summer pruning, to 5cm (2in) on sideshoots.

2 Thin spurs to avoid overcrowding, while the plant is dormant. This is only done on established plants, not young ones.

3 Remove the weakest and most congested spurs first, leaving those remaining well spaced.

4 Once the main stem has reached the required height, prune the main stem back to within 12mm (0.5in) of the old wood.

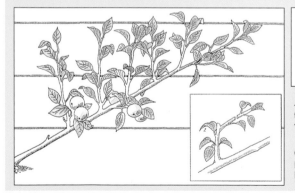

5 Prune sideshoots in late summer, once they are brown and woody at the base.

6 Left Prune to one leaf above the basal cluster of leaves, on all spurs.

PRUNING AN ESPALIER

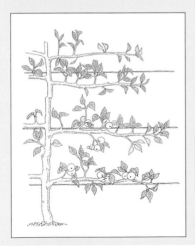

1 When the plant is dormant, thin out overcrowded spurs. This will only be needed on established espaliers.

2 In late summer, when this year's shoots are brown and woody, begin pruning. Cut back shoots over 23cm (9in) long, to three leaves above the basal cluster.

3 Cut sideshoots from spurs, back to one leaf above the basal cluster of leaves.

4 Cut back any secondary growth to one leaf from its base, in early autumn.

PRUNING A BUSH OR STANDARD APPLE OR PEAR TREE

The methods shown here are easy if pruning has been carried out regularly. They are suitable for bush and standard trees. If the flowers and fruit on your tree grow mainly in clusters along the shoots, follow the advice for spur pruning. If the fruit grows mainly on the tips of the shoots, follow the advice for pruning a tip bearer.

Bush apples are not difficult to prune and give a high yield.

BARK RINGING

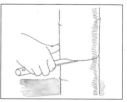

1 Bark ringing helps to reduce the vigour of a strong apple or pear, and may stimulate a poorly fruiting tree to produce a better crop. Make two cuts, deep enough to penetrate the bark and hard wood layer, in late spring.

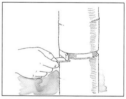

2 Remove the bark with the knife blade, around the tree.

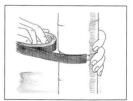

3 Wind waterproof tape around the wound to reduce the risk of disease. Remove when the wound heals.

SPUR PRUNING

1 While the tree is dormant, prune each branch in turn. Cut sideshoots to 2–6 buds.

2 Shorten the tip of the main shoot by one-third and one-quarter.

3 Thin spurs if needed. Cut out the weakest and remove others to leave spurs well-spaced and uncongested.

FRUIT & VEGETABLES

PRUNING A TIP BEARER

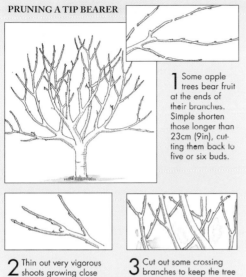

1 Some apple trees bear fruit at the ends of their branches. Simple shorten those longer than 23cm (9in), cutting them back to five or six buds.

2 Thin out very vigorous shoots growing close together.

3 Cut out some crossing branches to keep the tree open and uncluttered.

NICKING AND NOTCHING

You can reduce the vigour of a shoot by removing a small crescent of bark and hard wood, just below a bud. This will restrict the growth of the shoot above. This process is called nicking.

If you want to stimulate a branch to grow out, perhaps to fill in a gap, make a similar cut just above the bud. This is known as notching.

Apples grown on dwarfing rootstocks will make compact bushes or small trees, like this 'Sunset'. Ask your garden centre for advice.

THINNING AND ROOT PRUNING

To grow large apples and pears, thin overcrowded spurs in winter and thin overcrowded fruits in summer. If your fruit tree is too vigorous, try root pruning.

ROOT PRUNING

1 Root pruning when the tree is dormant, may help reduce its vigour. Make an arc around half of the tree, inside the spread of branches. Root prune only one half of the tree each year.

2 Dig a trench around half the tree, using the guide line.

3 Use a fork to expose deeper roots.

4 Saw through large exposed roots. Leave small, fibrous roots undamaged. Fill in with soil and firm back.

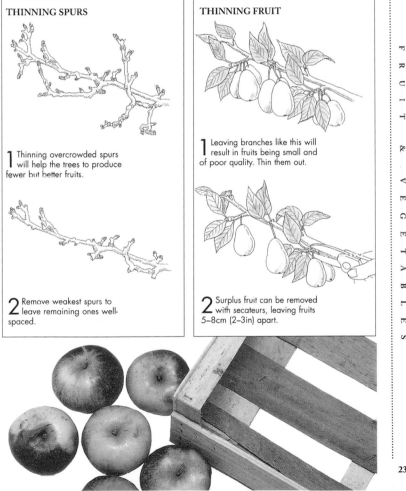

THINNING SPURS

1 Thinning overcrowded spurs will help the trees to produce fewer but better fruits.

2 Remove weakest spurs to leave remaining ones well-spaced.

THINNING FRUIT

1 Leaving branches like this will result in fruits being small and of poor quality. Thin them out.

2 Surplus fruit can be removed with secateurs, leaving fruits 5–8cm (2–3in) apart.

PROTECTING YOUR FRUIT

Apples and pears are prone to pests and diseases, so spraying is advisable for an unblemished crop. Strike a balance by using some non-toxic controls and spraying when the chemicals will not harm beneficial insects.

GREASE BANDING

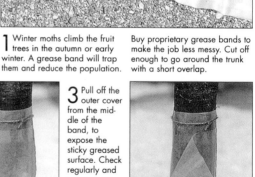

1 Winter moths climb the fruit trees in the autumn or early winter. A grease band will trap them and reduce the population.

Buy proprietary grease bands to make the job less messy. Cut off enough to go around the trunk with a short overlap.

2 Tie the bands into place at the top and bottom. Make sure that they are in close contact with the trunk.

3 Pull off the outer cover from the middle of the band, to expose the sticky greased surface. Check regularly and remove any debris which could act as a bridge over the grease.

PHEROMONE TRAPS

1 Pheromone traps work by attracting male insects to the scent of a female. They are available for codling moths and some other insects.

2 Place the pheromone on the sticky surface of the trap.

3 Hang the trap in the tree, so it can be checked regularly. Killing males will reduce the population as fewer females will be fertilized. Check traps twice a week, spraying when there are a lot of males around.

TERMS YOU MAY NEED TO KNOW

Sprays control pests should not be used when bees are pollinating the flowers. Make sure that you understand the following terms.
Bud burst is when tight buds are just expanding, **green cluster** when the flower buds are obvious, **pink bud** (white for pears) is when colour starts to show, and **petal fall** is when the petals of the first flowers start to drop.

Pink bud (apple)

Full flower

How to Grow Outdoor Grapes

There are several ways to grow outdoor grapes, but the Guyot system described here is one of the easiest.

FRUIT & VEGETABLES

FORMATIVE PRUNING

1 Prune the main shoot back to just three strong buds.

2 The first summer, let these shoots grow, tying them to grow vertically.

3 Next winter, lower the two strongest shoots and tie horizontally. Cut the upright shoot back to three buds. Next summer, tie in shoots growing vertically.

ESTABLISHED GUYOT PRUNING

1 Prune the central shoot back to three buds. Select two new shoots to shorten and tie in.

2 Cut out all other shoots. Bend over the young shoots and tie to the bottom wires.

3 New shoots grown on the bottom wire should be tied in to the other wires, so that they grow vertically.

4 Pinch out the growing tips to leaves above the top wire., and any sideshoots growing from shoots already carrying fruit.

Grapes can be very decorative fruit. This variety is 'Brandt'.

HOW TO GROW PEACHES AND NECTARINES

Peaches and nectarines are both treated in the same way. A fan-trained tree will give good results in all but mild areas. It is best to buy a ready-trained tree or consult a specialist book. The advice given here is for established bush and fan trees.

THINNING

Peaches and nectarines may need thinning to produce a bigger crop. Snip off surplus fruit, to leave just one fruit per cluster.

PRUNING A BUSH TREE

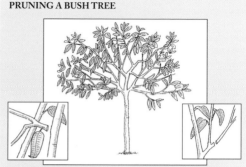

1 In early summer, cut out any dead or diseased branches. If the tree is congested, cut out some older branches.

2 Cut back any dying branches on a tree that has been fruiting for several years. Don't do this to more than one-quarter of the branches overall.

PRUNING A FAN TREE

1 Disbud young shoots, so they grow every 15cm (6in), once leaves emerge in the spring. Leave the bud at the base of the shoot alone, to carry fruit next year.

2 After harvesting, prune each shoot that has borne fruit. These are shoots developed from a bud left to grow from the base during spring pruning.

3 Tie this replacement shoot to the cane that supported the fruited shoot that has just been removed.

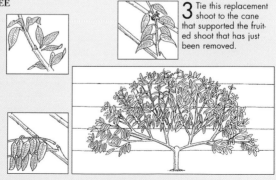

HOW TO GROW CURRANTS

Blackcurrants are easy to grow and prune. Red and white currants are also easy fruit to grow, but they are trained and pruned in a different way.

PLANTING

1 Plant in well-prepared ground to which fertilizer has been added. Plant at the same depth.

2 Plant 1.2–1.5m (4–5ft) apart and firm the soil well around the roots.

3 Straight after planting, cut back all the stems on a blackcurrant to the first or second bud above the ground. this stimulates new shoots to grow.

4 For red and white currants, prune off any sideshoots growing within 10–15cm (4–6in) of the soil, to produce a clear stem.

5 Prune back the main shoot by half, to an outward-facing bud. The next winter, reduce the length of all main shoots grown from last years pruning by half.

PRUNING AN ESTABLISHED BUSH

1 Prune blackcurrant bushes over three years old annually, ideally after harvesting or in the autumn. Cut any badly placed branches back to their origin.

2 Prune established red and white currant bushes annually. Shorten the tips of leading shoots to encourage new growth.

3 Prune each sideshoot from these branches to just one bud.

RASPBERRIES, BLACKBERRIES AND HYBRID BERRIES

PLANTING RASPBERRIES

1 Plant raspberries 45cm (18in) apart in a shallow trench with compost or manure added. Spread out the roots.

2 Firm the ground. Cut back to 25cm (10in). In mid summer, cut back original stem just above ground level and tie in.

PRUNING AND TRAINING RASPBERRIES

1 Train to wires stretched between posts. Space the wires 30cm (1ft) apart.

2 Prune summer-flowering varieties after fruiting. Cut back to ground level, canes that have fruited. Prune autumn-fruiting plants during the winter, cutting all canes back to ground level.

PRUNING BLACKBERRIES AND HYBRID BERRIES

1 Train fruit to wires stretched between posts, to make pruning easier.

2 Prune established plants after fruiting or when dormant. Cut back to the ground all canes that have fruited. Tie in the new shoots, spreading them out.

PLANTING BLACKBERRIES AND HYBRID BERRIES

Plant bare-rooted plants when dormant, from late autumn to early spring. Space them 2.4–5cm (8–15ft) apart depending on the variety.

HOW TO TRAIN RASPBERRIES

A post and rail system (see above) is simple and effective, although there are several other methods.

Space the wires at heights of 75cm (2.5ft). 90cm (3ft) and 1.5cm (5ft). Tie in the new shoots each season when 90cm (3ft) tall. Space them 10cm (4in) apart.

At the end of the season the canes will be above the top wire. Bend them over and tie down to the top wire. In spring, cut back to leave the canes 15cm (6in) above the top wire.

HOW TO GROW GOOSEBERRIES

Plant, feed and mulch goose-
berries as for blackcurrants,
prune after planting.

FORMATIVE PRUNING

Prune back shoots, after
planting, by half to stimulate plenty of branching.

PRUNING AN ESTABLISHED BUSH

1 Prune bushes over three years old annual-ly. In winter cut the tips of all main shoots back by half of the summer growth.

2 Prune each sideshoot from these branches back to 8cm (3in).

3 In early to mid summer cut sideshoots back to five leaves from their base. This will keep the bush more open and reduce the risk of diseases. Leave the main shoots intact during summer pruning.

242

HOW TO GROW STRAWBERRIES

Strawberries are very easy to grow, but always buy certified disease-free plants. If disease affects your plants, buy fresh plants. The method described is simple and reliable. Some varieties crop just once, while others produce several crops between early summer and mid autumn.

PLANTING

Strawberries need fertile soil so work plenty of compost or manure into the ground, removing all weeds before planting.

Rake in fertilizer, then plant 45cm (18in) apart, in rows 75cm (30in) apart.

The plants often arrive with bare roots. Spread the roots out on a mound, making sure that the crown is level with the surrounding surface, then return the soil.

Most plants are sold in pots. Water them an hour prior to planting out and plant at their original depth.

Remove flowers that appear during the first year. This allows the plants to get well established before bearing a crop of fruit.

ROUTINE CARE

1 The plants benefit from regular feeding. Sulphate of potash should be applied in early spring. If plants need a boost, apply sulphate of ammonia in mid spring.

2 Hoeing or hand weeding will keep down weeds.

3 Use special mats to keep the fruit clean. These must be in place as the fruits develop.

NEW PLANTS FROM RUNNERS

Spread out the runners in early to mid summer, and peg where there is a strong tuft of leaves into pots of compost plunged into the soil.

Pinch or cut off the runner just beyond the pegged-down point, but *do not sever the link with the parent plant.* Remove surplus runners not required.

Check after six weeks, and if the plant has rooted well, sever it from its parent.

4 It may be cheaper to lay a thick bed of straw around the plants.

HARVESTING AND STORING FRUIT

Fruit needs picking with special care if you plan to store or preserve it. Only pick perfect fruit—damaged or imperfect fruit should be used up when still fresh.

HOW TO STORE

These are some of the best ways to store some of the most popular fruits.

APPLES	Store wrapped; freeze as slices or purée; bottle as slices
APRICOTS	Freeze halved; bottle
BLACKBERRIES	Freeze whole; bottle
CHERRIES	Freeze after stoning (pitting); bottle
CURRANTS (BLACK, RED, WHITE)	Freeze whole; bottle
GOOSEBERRIES	Freeze whole or purée; bottle
PEACHES AND NECTARINES	Freeze after stoning (pitting); bottle
PEARS	Store wrapped
PLUMS	Freeze after stoning (pitting); bottle
RASPBERRIES	Freeze whole; bottle
STRAWBERRIES	Freeze whole or purée

PICKING AND STORING SOFT FRUIT

1 Pick strawberries carefully by the stalk to avoid bruising.

2 Pick raspberries as they become ripe. Pull them gently off the stalk, leaving the plug behind (pick with the stalk only if you will exhibit in a show.

3 Soft fruits freeze well. Remove stalks and hulls, then freeze the fruit whole, spread out on trays.

4 Once frozen, transfer the fruit to bags or boxes, and remove as much air as possible.

PICKING AND STORING APPLES AND PEARS

1 Apples and pears are ready for picking when the fruit comes away from the tree easily. Twist and remove the fruit with the stalk intact.

2 Bruised fruit does not store well. Line a basket with straw or paper and place the fruit in this as you harvest it.

3 Wrap each fruit individually in greaseproof paper, placing the fruit in the centre of a square of paper.

4 Fold two opposite corners over the fruit carefully.

5 Fold over the other two corners and place fruit in trays.

6 Right Keep in a well ventilated container in a cool but frost-free place.

FRUIT FACTS AT YOUR FINGERTIPS

Use this table as a quick reference guide for advice on the requirements and harvesting times for all the common fruits. The dates given are for popular varieties and methods of cultivation: these may vary for specific varieties and the weather. Always check the label or seek advice from the nurseryman about planting details, spacings and if pollinators are required.

NAME	SOIL AND SITE	HARVEST	REMARKS
APPLE	Any soil. Full sun. Avoid frost pockets	Late summer to late autumn	Regular pruning and spraying necessary for good crops
APRICOT	Well-drained soil, warm, sunny position. Frost protection	Mid and late summer	For small gardens choose a tree grafted on a very dwarfing rootstock
BLACKBERRY AND HYBRID BERRIES	Undemanding Avoid frost pockets	Mid summer to early autumn	Regular pruning and training are essential
BLACKCURRANT	Undemanding.	Mid and late summer	Annual pruning and feeding
BLUEBERRY	Only acid soils – pH 5.5 or less	Mid to late summer	Protection from birds may be necessary
CHERRY	Ordinary soil	Mid and late summer	To make cherry growing easy in a small garden, choose a self-fertile variety
FIG	Any soil, sunny position	Late summer and early autumn	It may be necessary to restrict root spread
GOOSEBERRY	Any soil. Best in full sun. Avoid frost pockets	Early and mid summer	Very prone to a form of mildew, so routine spraying may be necessary
GRAPE	Well-drained, fertile soil. Full sun	Early and mid autumn	Dessert grapes are best grown in a greenhouse

NAME	SOIL AND SITE	HARVEST	REMARKS
KIWI	Any soil, warm, sunny position	Mid autumn	Needs a male plant to pollinate the female fruiting variety
PEACH AND NECTARINE	Fertile soil, sunny position	Mid summer to early autumn depending on variety	Except in the warmest areas, best grown as a fan against a warm wall
PEAR	Fertile soil, sunny position	Early autumn to early winter	Will need a pollinator. Seek advice for your variety
PLUM, GAGE, DAMSON	Fertile soil, sunny position	Late summer to late autumn	Avoid early varieties in cold areas (blossom is often damaged by frost)
RASPBERRY	Fertile soil, sunny position	Mid summer to mid autumn	Prune and train annually
RED CURRANT AND WHITE CURRANT	Any soil if well-drained	Mid and late summer	Can be trained as a cordon
STRAWBERRY	Fertile soil in full sun	Early summer to autumn	Propagate new plants regularly

SUPPLIERS

UK

GARDEN EQUIPMENT AND SUPPLIES

Axminster Power Tool Centre
Chard Street, Axminster
Devon EX13 5HU
Telephone: 01297 33656
Fax: 01297 35242

Chase Organics (GB) Ltd
(fertilizers)
Riverdean Estate
Mousley Road
Hersham
Surrey KT12 4RG
Telephone: 01932 253666

Greevale Farm Ltd
(Fisons Origins Range)
Wonastow Road
Monmouth
Gwent NP5 3XX

Humber Fertilisers
PO Box 27
Stoneferry
Hull
Humberside HU8 8DQ

P G Horticulture
(modules)
Street Farm
Thornham Magna, Eye
Suffolk IP23 8HB

SEEDS

B&T World Seeds
Whitnell House
Fiddington
Bridgwater
Somerset TA5 1JE

D T Brown & Co Ltd
Station Road
Poulton-le-Fylde
Blackpool
Lancashire FY6 7HX
Telephone: 01253 882371

Chase Organics (GB) Ltd
(see Garden Equipment and Supplies)

Chiltern Seeds
Bortree Stile
Ulverston
Cumbria LA12 7PB
Telephone: 01229 581137

Cowcombe Farm Herbs
Gipsy Lane
Chalford, Stroud
Gloucestershire GL6 8HP

Samuel Dobie & Sons Ltd
Broomhill Way
Torquay
Devon TQ2 7QW
Telephone: 01803 616281

King Crown Quality Seeds
Monks Farm, Pantling Lane
Coggleshall Road
Kelvedon
Essex CO5 9PG

Seymour's Selected Seeds
Abacus House
Station Yard
Needham Market
Suffolk IP6 8AS

Stewart's (Nottingham) Ltd
3 George Street
Nottingham
NG1 3BH
Telephone: 0115 947 6338

NURSERIES

Craigieburn Classic Plants
Craigieburn House
by Moffat
Dumfriesshire DG10 9LF
Telephone: 01683 386286

Crankan Nurseries
New Mill
Penzance
Cornwall

Hazeldene Nursery
Dean Street, East Farleigh
Maidstone
Kent ME15 0PS

The Herb Nursery
Grange Farm, Main Street
Thistleton
Rutland LE15 7RE
Telephone: 01572 767658

Holden Clough Nursery
Holden
Bolton by Bowland
Nr Clitheroe
Lancashire BB7 4PF
Telephone: 01200 447615

Marle Place Plants & Gardens
Marle Place
Brenchley
Nr Tonbridge
Kent TN12 7HS

Naked Cross Nurseries
Waterloo Road
Corfe Mullen
Wimborne
Dorset BH21 3SR
Telephone: 01202 693256

Old Manor Nurseries
South Leverton
Retford
Nottinghamshire DN22 0BX

Pennine Nurseries
Shelley
Huddersfield
Yorkshire HD8 8LG
Telephone: 01484 605511

The Plant Place
63/67 Camberwell Road
London SE5 8TR
Telephone: 0171 252 6565

Pocock's Nurseries
Dandy's Ford Lane
Sherfield English
Romsey
Hampshire SO51 6FT
Telephone: 01794 23514

Rumwood Nurseries
Langley
Maidstone
Kent ME17 3ND
Telephone: 01622 861477

St Bridget's Nurseries Ltd
Old Rydon Lane
Exeter
Devon EX2 7JY
Telephone: 01392 873672

Stillingfleet Lodge Nurseries
Stillingfleet
Yorkshire YO4 6HW

Stydd Nursery
Stoneygate Lane, Ribchester
Nr Preston
Lancashire PR3 3YN
Telephone: 01254 878797

Sussex County Gardens
Newhaven Road
Kingston, Nr Lewes
E Sussex BN7 3NE

Thyme House Nursery
Manea March
Cambridgeshire
Telephone: 01354 680412

Walter Blom & Son Ltd
Coombelands Nurseries
Leavesdon, Watford
Hertfordshire WD2 7BH

GARDEN STRUCTURES AND ORNAMENTS

Agriframes Ltd
Charlwoods Road
East Grinstead
W Sussex RH19 2HG

Capital Garden Products Ltd
Hurst Green
Etchingham
E Sussex TN19 7QU
Telephone: 01580 201092

PONDS AND FOUNTAINS

JNS
21 Greenside
Prestwood
Buckinghamshire HP6 0SE

Pondliners
Freepost 62
Nicolson Link
Clifton Moor
York YO1 1SS
Telephone: 01904 691169
Fax: 01904 691133

Reef Aquatics
Catfoot Lane
Lambley
Nottinghamshire NG4 4DQ
Telephone: 01602 676100
Fax: 01602 673266

Stapeley Water Gardens Ltd
London Road
Nantwich
Cheshire
Telephone: 01270 628111

The Very Interesting Rock Co
PO Box 27
Leamington Spa
Warwickshire
Telephone: 01926 313465

FENCING

Lemar
Harrowbrook Industrial Estate
Hinckley
Leicestershire LE10 3DJ
Telephone: 01455 637077

Rob Turner
Unit 16, Moor's Yard
High Street
Stalham
Norfolk NR12 9AN
Telephone: 01692 580091

Greenhouses, Sunrooms and Conservatories

Alite Metals
7 Maze Street
Barton Hill
Bristol BS5 9TE
Telephone: 01272 553100

Archwood Greenhouses
Robinwood
Goodrich
Herefordshire HR9 6HT
Telephone: 01600 890125

Regal National Garden Building Centre
Cromford Road
Langley Mill
Nottinghamshire NG16 4EB
Telephone: 01733 530428

AUSTRALIA

GARDEN CENTRES

Swanes
490 Galston Road
Dural NSW 2158
Telephone: (02) 651 1322

Michele Shennen's
Garden Centres
44 Old Barrenjoey Road
Avalon NSW 2107
Telephone: (02) 918 6738

Bond's Nursery
363 Military Road
Mosman NSW 2088
Telephone: (02) 953 3700

Sherringhams Nurseries Pty Ltd
299a Lane Cove Road
North Ryde NSW 2113
Telephone: (02) 888 3133

Rast Brothers
29 Kissing Point Road
Turramurra NSW 2074
Telephone: (02) 44 2134

Tropigro
PO Box 39827
Winnellie NT 0821
Telephone:(089) 84 3200

SUPPLIERS

Gippsland Growers
125 Sutton Street
Warragul VIC 3920
Telephone: (056)23 6718

Warner's Nurseries Pty Ltd
395 Warrigal Road
Burwood VIC 3125
Telephone: (03) 808 2321

**Richgro Horticultural
Products**
Lot 186 Acourt Road
Canningvale WA 6155
Telephone: (09) 455 1323

SEEDS

Australian Seed Co
5 Rosedale Ave
Hazelbrook NSW 2779
Telephone: (047) 586132

Ellison Horticultural
PO Box 365
Nowra NSW 2541
Telephone: (044) 21 4255

Harvest Seed Company
PO Box 544
Newport Beach NSW 2106
Telephone: (02) 997 2277

Diggers Seeds
Box 300
Dromana VIC 3936
Telephone: (059) 87 1877

NEW ZEALAND

NURSERIES

Big Trees
Main Road, Coatesville
Auckland
Telephone: (09) 415 9983

Golden Coast Nurseries
Main Road, North Paekakariki
Telephone: 292 8556

Kent's Nurseries
Cr. Ferguson Drive & Ranfurly St
Trentham
Telephone: (4) 528 3389

Rainbow Tree Nursery
Cooper Road
Ramarama
Sth Auckland

GARDENING CENTRES

**California Green World
Garden Centre**
139 Park Road
Miramar
Wellington
Telephone: (4) 388 3260

Palmer's Garden World
Cr. Shore &Orakei Roads
Remeura
Auckland
Telephone: (09) 524 4038

Zeniths
92 Epuni Street
Lower Hutt
Telephone: (04) 566 1493

GARDEN POOL CENTRES

**Garden Statues and
Ornaments**
Hewletts Road
Mt Maunganui
Telephone: (07) 575 5797

STATUARY

Chase Organics (GB) Ltd
see UK Garden Equipment and
Suppliers.

GAZEBOS

Wellington Sheds & Carports
Cr. Petone Esplanade & Hutt Rd
Petone
Wellington
Telephone: (04) 568 9626

INDEX

ACKNOWLEDGEMENTS

The author and publishers would like to thank the staff and students of Capel Manor Horticultural and Environmental Centre, Bullsmoor Lane, Enfield, Middlesex for their cooperation in the photographing of this book.

The publishers would also like to thank the following: Gardena for generously lending most of the tools used in photography; Wyevale Cramphorn Garden Centres plc for lending a wide range of gardening equipment; Stapely Water Gardens for lending the pictures on page 155; and Lotus Water Products Ltd for donating the pre-formed pool featured on page 154.

Photographs are by Paul Forrester, John Freeman, Peter McHoy and Lucy Mason.